"MICHELLE'S BOOK IS BEAUTIFULLY WRITTEN, heartfelt and emotive. It is such an engaging and absorbing read that I felt myself welling up a few times, which is a rarity for me. This heartbreaking story of a mother losing her son and how she found hope and meaning from the tragedy, is surprisingly inspiring and uplifting. It is a wonderful tribute to her special boy, Dustin, who's spirit lives on and shines through in this story."

-Glenn Harrold, Author of *Meditation for Cosmic Ordering* and *A Guided Meditation for Relaxation, Well-Being, and Healing*

Huffman Legend

Miss Me but Let Me Go

Image Courtesy of Erin Murphy

Michelle Huffman

BALBOA
PRESS
A DIVISION OF HAY HOUSE

Balboa Press books may be ordered through booksellers or by contacting:

Balboa Press
A Division of Hay House
1663 Liberty Drive
Bloomington, IN 47403
www.balboapress.com
1 (877) 407-4847

Print information available on the last page.

ISBN: 978-1-5043-8799-6 (sc)
ISBN: 978-1-5043-8800-9 (e)

Balboa Press rev. date: 11/30/2017

Image Courtesy of Eska Paumier

Please support the
Dustin Huffman Memorial Scholarship
with your tax deductible donation today.
www.DustinHuffmanMemorialScholarship.org

Join us the third Saturday of August each year for the

RUN FAST WINGED 5K

Walkers welcome, and their dogs too☺

The story is true, however, some of the names have been
changed to respect the privacy of those involved.

The illustrations in this book can be viewed in full color
photographs at HuffmanLegend.com and are available for
purchase in prints as well as other mediums such as t-shirts.

TABLE OF CONTENTS

This book is dedicated to:

Dustin Marshall Huffman

08/21/1991 – 06/30/2009

PREFACE

H UFFMAN LEGEND IS THE TRUE story of how my incredible son helps me to heal my grief, from the other side.

Dustin was charismatic, funny and kind, and finished his junior year as a hero when he won a gold medal in track at the state championship.

When school let out for the summer, he got a job at a local tree company. I argued against it because of a premonition I had, but no one would take me serious.

A few weeks later, while working at Gretchen's Lock, an area famous for being haunted, he fell one-hundred feet off a rocky cliff and my baby was gone. He was only seventeen.

It was a mother's worst nightmare. I was destroyed. Tranquilizers and tequila became a way of life, until a psychic said that it made him sad to see me cry all the time, because it made him feel like he broke me. It was time for a change and I replaced medication with meditation.

Once I was sober, I started to notice signs. Lots of them! Mysterious phenomena that defied logical explanation and that continue on a regular basis.

One day, I was crying hysterically as I walked down the hallway to the bedrooms. I stopped in front of his room and screamed his name at the top of my lungs, "DUSTIN!"

Suddenly, I could smell his cologne. It stunned me and was comforting, but I didn't know what to think. It was just too much to process at the time. I know now that he heard my plea and came to comfort me. Since then, I have been blessed with many signs which have helped to heal my grief and launched me on a spiritual journey that changed my life forever.

Be open to the signs your loved ones send or you just might not recognize them for what they are. They want you to know that they are waiting for you.

I no longer believe in coincidences. I do, however, believe in synchronicity – events connected by meaning. According to the Akashic Records, "Synchronicity happens when you align with the flow of the universe, rather than insisting the universe flow your way."

CHAPTER ONE

Image Courtesy of Nick J. Cool, The Image Works Photographic

GO BIG OR GO HOME

T RANQUILIZERS AND TEQUILA HELPED TO numb the pain and had become a way of life to deal with the grief. My doctor prescribed the Ativan I so desperately needed, and Patron was readily available at the local liquor store.

Sleep was often interrupted by screams of anguish because of the night terrors that haunted me. My eyes were red and swollen from crying—and not just random bouts of crying; we're talking sobbing uncontrollably on a daily basis for well over a year.

I could barely function, let alone go back to work, and my self-destructive lifestyle was taking its toll on my health—physically, mentally, emotionally and spiritually. Life had no meaning, and I just wanted it to end.

My husband, Dave, tried to help, but I rejected his attempts to console me. I called him names and told him that I hated him. I blamed him for our loss, and there was nothing he could say or do that would change my mind.

Dave was at a loss on how to help me, so occasionally he called in reinforcements. Friends and family came to try and help. They expressed their love and concern in an effort to ease the grief that held me hostage. When it came down to it, there was really nothing anyone could do. How do you fix a broken heart?

One early morning I was sitting in my recliner in the family room drinking a cup of hot coffee while trying to pull myself together. My long, dark, unkempt hair was draped over my slouching shoulders, hiding most of my face. I was just staring into space, still in a state of disbelief.

"Oh, it hasn't been a year yet," was something I had heard often from others doing their best to console me—as if once a year was reached everything would magically get better. Well it wasn't better. In fact, it was worse because of having that expectation.

The room was quiet except for the humming sound of the computer. Dave was in his own world catching up with emails and checking out the latest news. The silence was broken when the phone rang.

"Hello," I answered. It was Dustin's friend, Eden.

Eden camped with her family at Timashamie Family Campground, where she and Dustin met. Dustin was only eight when we first went there. She was a few years older—your typical tomboy with wavy brown hair and mischievous dark brown eyes.

Timashamie was Dustin's favorite place in the whole world, and as long as he checked in with me regularly, he could run around and play on his own. The rule was that he had to have his walkie-talkie and a friend with him. Most often that friend was Eden.

The two of them spent countless hours swimming, fishing, hiking, and playing in the creek. Timashamie was a kid's paradise.

"Hi Michelle. How are you?" she asked.

Sweet memories of the past came flooding back when I heard Eden's voice. It was hard to believe that six years had passed since we left Timashamie. I hadn't talked to her in quite a while but I always enjoyed hearing about the adventures she and Dustin shared.

After a deep sigh, I replied, "I'm okay." My heart was hurting and she could probably hear it in my voice. I expected some generic message of consolation from her, but I didn't expect what I was about to hear next.

"I have a message from Dustin," she said. My heart was pounding and I couldn't speak, so I just listened. She continued by saying, "I talked to a friend of mine who told me that he wants me to relay a message to you and Dave."

She certainly had my attention now. I implored her to go on, "Really, please tell me. What did he say?"

"Dustin wants you to know that he's okay and that he's sending you the orbs as signs to let you know this."

I had no idea what an "Orb" was, but I'd seen several pictures on Facebook posted by Dustin's friends that had unusual glowing balls of light in them. There were three orbs, and they all had something to do with him in some way or another. I had initially assumed these to be photographic anomalies, but now I wasn't so sure.

Eden finished by saying, "Dustin wants you to know that it hurts his heart to see you cry all the time because he feels like he broke you."

My eyes welled up with tears and I started sobbing uncontrollably. It was devastating to be told that my behavior was hurting my son on the other side. I didn't even realize this was possible, but then again, how could I?

Parents are not supposed to outlive their children. It's just not the natural order of things, and many parents never get over it. I know I haven't, nor will I ever get over losing my son, but after talking to Eden, I knew that somehow I had to learn to deal with the loss of my beautiful boy in a more productive manner. I had to get a hold of myself!

I thanked Eden for calling and hung up the phone. Quite shaken, I went to the bathroom to splash some water on my face. My reflection in the mirror showed a haggard and beaten-down woman. The bottle of Ativan on the counter was a reminder that this was not what Dustin would have wanted.

I wanted to live the life that he would want me to live, and I knew that he would want me to be happy. I wanted to live a life that would make him as proud of me as I was of him--a life that would honor his memory.

First and foremost, I needed to get off the medication and quit drinking. In the weeks to come, I got back into shape by working out, which also helped to accelerate my detox. I tried to keep a positive attitude, and it wasn't long before I was feeling a little better.

Forgiving Dave for what I saw as his part in Dustin's accident and accepting that it was God's will would take a little longer, but it was critical to the healing process. It wasn't Dave's fault, and I knew that Dustin would not want me to blame him. He loved his dad and wanted both of us to be happy.

Dustin's message was clear. He not only wanted me to be happy— he was taking an active role in helping me to help others by using his example. I am going to honor his memory by doing just that and living my life to the fullest.

Like Dustin used to say,

"Go big or go home!"

CHAPTER TWO

I KNEW

D USTIN HAD THAT ALL-AMERICAN LOOK, usually dressing in his American Eagle jeans and t-shirt. He wore Nike tennis shoes that were custom ordered with "HUFFMAN" embossed on the backs of them. His short, dark brown hair made his bright blue eyes pop, and a dimple on his right cheek accentuated an ornery grin. His charismatic nature lit up any room he entered.

I fixed up the basement so that Dustin would have a cool place to hang out with his friends. This wasn't some dark, musty hole in ground—sunlight flooded the basement, since it was on ground level on the east end. He worked out in the sun room with weights and would occasionally take his frustrations out on the punching bag. The canvas is spotted with blood stains from when he beat it without using his gloves.

A picture of Dale Earnhardt hung on the wall, and the black and white checkered tile on the floor added to the NASCAR theme. It went well with the red and black theme for Salem's school colors. Dustin was all about his school.

He sure never had a shortage of friends. Kids were always coming and going, and it was difficult to keep up with all the names. And I just loved that our house was the place to be!

The kids lounged on the overstuffed, red leather couches, playing Xbox or watching their favorite shows on a large flat screen TV. Other times they played pool on the ball and claw oak table that was trimmed in red felt. Dozens of kids gathered every year when it was time for a super bowl party. It was wonderful to have a place for him and his friends to hang out: a place where I knew he was safe.

When Dustin was in sixth grade, he brought a new friend home named Kyle. Kyle looked like he could be Scandinavian, with his big blue eyes, blonde hair, and lanky stature. The boys got along great.

"Hello Mrs. Huffman," Kyle said with a genuine smile when we first met. His manners were impeccable, and you couldn't ask for a nicer kid, but for whatever reason that I couldn't explain, I was uncomfortable with Dustin playing with him. Kyle was a great kid with a huge heart, but still I discouraged the friendship. I even felt guilty about it because there seemed to be no reason for it. It was just a feeling.

We hadn't seen Kyle in years, but once they were in high school, he and Dustin rekindled their friendship. He even got Dustin a job with his family's business. When I found out, the hair went up on the back of my neck and I got a knot in my stomach.

"No", I screamed without hesitation. "I don't want you working there!" Fear and panic overwhelmed me, and I fought against Dustin taking the job. He was the most competent person I had ever known, so it wasn't that I questioned his ability to do the work. There was something about this job that was very unsettling to me. I just did not know why. Unfortunately, my husband sided with Dustin.

Dave loved Dustin more than anything in the world and beamed with pride at the very thought of him. He was such a pushover for his Dustin that he could never tell him no for anything. Dave never enforced bedtimes and would give in to his every whim.

I remember a time when Dave went to the store at ten o' clock at night to get Dustin Cool Ranch Doritos. We had the original Doritos, but that wasn't what Dustin wanted, and Dustin always got what he wanted.

We both spoiled him in our own way, and now we are so very glad we did. He was honest and hardworking, and everyone knew that if they needed help, Dustin would be there, no matter what time of day or night—it didn't matter if it was for helping someone on a job or lending an ear when a friend needed to talk. He deserved to be spoiled, but letting him work at the tree service was not something I went along with.

But Dustin loved his new job and looked forward to going every day. Then, one morning, he came back home after showing up at the shop for work to find that there was no one else there. They didn't even call him to let him know work was cancelled. He had only worked there a few weeks, and it had happened several times, so it was getting frustrating.

I was cleaning the garage when Dustin got back home, so I asked him to help me. It was the perfect opportunity to talk to him about this job that I so didn't want him working. At one point I emphatically said to him, "I told you to get another job!"

Dustin replied defensively, "Well you won't help me." He was only sixteen and didn't have any experience looking for work, so he was a little unsure about himself in this regard. This seemed odd because he was usually confident about most things. And he was confident about most things because he usually excelled in most things. His classmates even referred to him as "HUFFMAN LEGEND,"

I seized the opportunity and quickly marched into the house to get on the computer to search the online classifieds for jobs in our area. There were very few jobs listed since Salem is a small town with a declining economy, and even fewer jobs that would be appropriate for a teenager, but there was one.

I dialed the number for Shoemaker Dairy Farm, then held the phone up to Dustin's ear and firmly said, "Talk." He told them he was calling about the ad in the newspaper and talked a little about himself. They scheduled him for an interview, and I will never forget how happy I was when he got the job.

Dustin loved his job on the farm. He often invited friends to go with him, and on one occasion asked me and my husband to go so he could show us what he did. Dustin warned us that we would need to wear our boots because it had rained earlier in the day.

After arriving at the farm, we parked the car in the driveway and crossed the muddy yard to the barn. Stalls lined the length of the walls, with another two rows running back to back down the center of the building. There were dozens of hungry calves who were happy to see Dustin.

We proceeded to a small room in the front corner of the building where Dustin prepared the formula. After filling the bottles, he put them in holders suspended from the gates on the stalls at just the right height for the calves to drink from. He often reached in to give them a loving pat before going on to the next stall. Dustin loved these babies and even gave many of them names.

After feeding the calves, Dustin went outside to the pasture. There he yelled out, "Bambi!" She was his favorite. He had bottle fed her by hand because she was so tiny when she was born. They developed a very special bond, and she would always come running when he called for her. After a proper greeting, he lovingly stroked her face. The rest of the cows ran to join them when he started throwing hay over the fence.

Dustin worked hard five days a week. Quite often he would have to carry a newborn calf in from the field to the barn. They can weigh sixty to seventy pounds. The job was demanding, but he could handle it. Dustin had an amazing work ethic and the strength and endurance to perform his duties well.

When school started in the fall, Dustin cut his hours back to a few evenings a week, but come spring it was time for track, so we told him to quit his job and focus on running. It was a no-brainer. He was scholarship material and we knew it. He had a stride as graceful as a gazelle. His Spanish teacher, who was actually Spanish, said to me, "I used to love to watch him run. He run like a beautiful deer."

Dustin had gone to the 2007 state championship as an alternate when he was a freshman and was determined to go back again his sophomore year, but as a main runner. Everything was going great, and the coach had high hopes for his team, until Dustin and one of his teammates were in a motorcycle accident.

Dustin and his friend had been riding their dirt bikes on a figure-eight-shaped track, and having a great time doing it. Unfortunately, the two collided and came crashing down when they met up in mid-air on the hill in the center of the track. They both sustained injuries that prevented them from running for the rest of the season. Any hope of going to state for that year was gone. The coach was not happy, but both boys went through physical therapy and were in good shape to run again by their junior year.

Dustin loved track and wanted to run, but he was reluctant to give up his job. He had gotten used to having extra money. I encouraged him to quit by saying, "I don't want you to worry about anything. Don't worry about your truck, money for gas, movies, or whatever. We will take care of you. You just *run fast.*"

He did just that and had a phenomenal season. As a payoff, in June of 2009, he and his teammates competed for the state championship in the Ohio High School Athletic Association (OHSAA)! It was held at the Jesse Owens stadium at the Ohio State University, home of the Buckeyes.

Dave and I left for Columbus as soon as I got off work Friday afternoon. We were almost there when Dustin called. The track team had arrived there several hours earlier. He was so excited because the team was staying at the Blackwell on campus. It was a very upscale and very expensive hotel.

When I answered my phone, Dustin exclaimed, "Mom, you and Dad have to stay here at the Blackwell! They only have one room left."

I replied by saying, "I'm sorry, Dustin, but we can't. We already have a hotel booked. Besides, we can't afford the Blackwell."

"But Mom" he argued, "This place is so cool, and it is really close to the track."

I told Dustin that we would be checking into our hotel soon and meeting up with him afterwards. He expressed his disappointment, telling me that I was cheap, and said goodbye.

We had just pulled into our hotel parking lot when the phone rang again. When I answered it, Dustin pleaded with me, "Mom, you have to come to the Blackwell! They only have one room left, and I have it reserved for you and Dad. Please."

He was very insistent, making it difficult to say no to him. Besides, what teenager actually wants his parents to stay in the same hotel with them and their friends? Dave and I decided that if it was that important to him, we would cancel the reservation we already had and stay at the Blackwell.

Dustin was waiting for us when we arrived. He led us to the counter in the lobby to make sure we got checked in. Afterwards we took our bags to the room where he showed us all the cool amenities that the Blackwell had to offer.

The room was tastefully decorated and bright with a great view of the campus. Fancy shampoos and soaps were provided as well as two very plush robes. It definitely was a nice hotel. A little later, we went to dinner with Dustin before he left to join his teammates.

The following day we met up with Dustin at the Jesse Owens Stadium. It had a capacity of 10,000, and it was a full house. There was a massive turnout of friends and family who came in support of these talented young athletes. It was interesting to meet the different people from all over the state. I even ran into a young girl who went to school in western Ohio where my cousin taught.

Mostly, it was so very exciting to be there to watch Dustin run. He was fulfilling his dream of going to state. His team did very well in the preliminaries and qualified for the finals. The next day would be the day they had been waiting for—the day they had trained so hard for.

Once again, Dave and I returned to the stadium to watch our Dustin run. After buying a t-shirt to remember the event, we found our way to the bleachers and sat down. There were a lot of events before the 800-meter relay that Dustin and his teammates would compete in, but the moment finally came.

The race began when the starter pistol rang out. Dustin was running the third leg, so he waited patiently while his teammates ran the first two legs of the race. He was on his mark and ready to go as he stared down at his shoes. He had used a Sharpie marker the night before to write "RUN" on his left shoe and "FAST" on his right one for motivation.

Dustin leapt to his feet and took off as his teammate approached him. It was a smooth handoff, and Dustin was off and running. He turned the curve and kicked it into high gear. The commentators went crazy and said, "Wow, this is cracking up. Man, but Salem is making up the ground now. Look at that move! This is a great leg for Salem. This is the deciding leg!"

Dustin blasted from fourth to first place in the straightaway. He approached the next curve, where he handed the baton off to his teammate running the fourth leg, who crossed the finish line in first place!

They did it! They brought a gold medal home to Salem, Ohio. They won first place in the 800-meter relay at the 2009 OHSAA Championship.

When the race was over, Dustin's coach was approached by several college scouts. They wanted to know who this kid was. They wanted Dustin.

The coach just smiled and said, "Sorry guys, you'll have to come back next year. He's only a junior." The coach was happy about having Dustin on the team for another year. He was really coming into his own.

Dustin finished his junior year as a hero. Now that school was out for the summer and track was over, it was time to get back to work. Mrs. Shoemaker was very anxious for him to return to his job on the farm because he was such a good worker, and because she loved him, just like everyone did— even the animals.

Several weeks went by before I figured out that Dustin had gone back to work for the tree company instead of the dairy farm. He and his dad knew how I felt about him working there, so they tried to keep it a secret from me.

I overheard them talking on the phone about it, so I confronted my husband and a heated argument ensued. I pleaded with him, "I don't want Dustin working there!" but Dave couldn't tell his son no, and he was not going to give in to me.

A few minutes later, Dustin came strolling in through the door, and then it was two against one. I didn't stand a chance, especially since there was no reason for my attitude except my gut feeling. They thought I was being ridiculous.

Dustin retreated into his hangout in the basement. I was furious and scared. I turned to my husband and asked in desperation, "Do you really think Dustin is going to be okay working there?

Dave just smiled and said, "He'll be fine."

About a week later, I was sitting in my recliner having a small glass of wine. Friday night was finally here, and I could enjoy a relaxing evening at home. I always looked forward to weekends, since working full time left me little time for myself.

I'd just finished an amazing dinner of filet mignon, asparagus, and strawberries. I was feeling great, and in the best shape I'd been in since my Army days, thirty years earlier. Working out with a personal trainer and eating healthy was paying off.

I was just sitting there, when suddenly, and for no apparent reason, I started to feel weak and so very tired. I got up to go to my room to lie down, but collapsed after only a few steps. My husband came running when he heard the big thud. He found me crumpled on the floor, unable to talk or move.

My brother, Mike, who we jokingly call Uncle Buck, was on the front porch talking on his cell phone when Dave yelled to him for help, "Buck, your sister fell!"

Uncle Buck came running into the house and helped Dave pick me up off the floor and get me back in my recliner. Dave asked me if I wanted to go lie down. I nodded in approval, so Dave and my brother each got on either side of me to help me to my room. We made it to the kitchen when my body went completely limp. They could no longer hold me, so they helped guide me gently down onto the kitchen floor.

It was so strange. I remember having body rushes and feeling hot and then cold, and very nauseous. The only sounds coming from my mouth were complete gibberish. I was paralyzed and helpless.

At one point I felt as if I had left my body and could actually see myself lying on the floor. Time seemed to slow down, and the scene was surreal. I was totally aware of and understood everything Dave and Buck were saying, but I couldn't speak or move at all. It was obvious that I needed medical attention.

My brother picked me up and carried me to the car. We only lived a few blocks away from the hospital, so they could get me there much quicker by car than an ambulance could even get to our house. We pulled up to the emergency room entrance and my brother ran in to get a wheelchair. He returned with one and placed my limp body in the chair and wheeled me in.

Triage took me in right away. They asked if I had been drinking because I appeared to be inibriated. My husband told them about the small glass of wine I had drunk. It was obvious they didn't believe him when they rolled their eyes.

The staff was surprised to find out the results of the toxicology screening. It confirmed that there were no drugs and next to no alcohol in my system. They knew something was definitely wrong with me now. My blood pressure had plummeted to 48/35, which is coma level and why I had no motor control. I was quickly admitted with many more tests to follow.

The next morning, I woke up when a nurse came in to take my blood pressure. It was still very low, but I was out of the danger zone and had regained control of my body. I recalled my experience on the kitchen floor and wondered if that's how coma patients feel; totally aware and totally helpless.

Later that morning, a middle-aged gentleman in a lab coat walked into the room. It was Dr. Clark. He had been the family physician for the Huffman's for many years, and was an excellent doctor. He genuinely cares about his patients, and he is so very easy to talk to.

Dr. Clark admitted he was totally baffled as to why my blood pressure had plummeted the way it did. I'd had no previously known health conditions, and none of the test results indicated that anything was wrong with me. He even said, "The EKG shows you have the heart of an eighteen-year-old athlete." I was fifty-one years old at the time.

My doctor scheduled my release for later that afternoon, and I spent the next few days in bed at home. On Monday I called off work for the first time in over a year because I was still so very weak. Tuesday wasn't much better, but I had to get back to work, so I forced myself to get up.

I put the coffee on and got dressed. The aroma of the brewing coffee was invigorating and just what I needed. I poured a cup and sat down to drink it when I heard Dustin in the next room. I looked up to see him heading for the front door to leave for work.

He reached for the door handle as I called out to him, "Dustin!" He looked back at me and I finished by saying, "Be careful. I love you!"

Being a typical teenage boy, he cocked his head and rolled his eyes with a smile and replied, "I love you too, Mom." Then he was out the door.

A few minutes later I left for work. It was a struggle to get through the morning. I just really wanted to go home and go back to bed.

Shortly after lunch the phone rang. It was my husband. He was hysterical and I couldn't understand him. "What?" I asked, "What are you saying?" He repeated himself. I'm pretty sure I understood him the second time, but I couldn't wrap my head around it. I asked him again, "What? Hun. I can't understand you!"

He repeated himself again: "He's dead. Dustin is dead!"

I screamed in a state of denial, "No! No! No!" I dropped the phone and almost collapsed. My co-workers came running into my office to see what was wrong. Everyone was in a state of disbelief when I told them what my husband said.

My boss insisted he take me home, saying I was in no shape to drive myself and someone else could pick up my car later. The twenty-minute commute seemed to take forever. I just kept saying over and over again, "It's a mistake. It's a mistake. It has to be a mistake."

As we drove up the street toward my house, we could see dozens of kids gathered in the front lawn. It was then that reality sank in. I started sobbing uncontrollably and said, "Oh my God! No! My baby can't be gone!"

It was raining when Dustin and his fellow employees arrived at the job site. They sat in the truck for almost an hour while they waited it out. Finally, it quit raining so they could get busy.

Dustin and Kyle worked for several hours cleaning up brush before it was time for their noon break. They sat in the truck listening to their favorite country songs while they ate their lunches. Ironically, one of the last songs Dustin listened to, according to his iTunes record, was: "Everybody Wants to Go To Heaven," by Kenny Chesney.

> Everybody wants to go to heaven,
> Have a mansion high above the clouds.
> Everybody want to go to heaven,
> But nobody wants to go now.

After lunch they had to wait until their supervisor was done dropping limbs before they could do clean-up detail. This is known as down time. Instead of just sitting there waiting, they decided to go exploring.

The terrain was treacherous, with cliffs hanging over a steep rocky hillside one hundred and fifty feet down to Beaver Creek. They were kids just having fun, kids who were at the age when they think they are invincible.

The rappelling gear they wore allowed them to navigate up and down the steep hillsides, and the view was amazing. Dustin was on one cliff looking over to see Kyle on another one across the way. They had traded phones earlier so they could take pictures of each other. A picture found on Dustin's phone shows him smiling from ear to ear. He was having a great adventure, and he was so very happy.

After exploring for a while, Dustin returned to the worksite and helped to adjust the outriggers. About five minutes later, Kyle returned to the top to tell the supervisor that Dustin had fallen.

Dustin had fallen off of a rocky cliff. The dirt path that led to the edge of the cliff was covered with wet leaves. The trail from Dustin's boots showed how he had skidded downward, unable to stop, before being launched over the cliff and plummeting a hundred feet to the ground below.

Kyle told us that he got to him as fast as he could and tried to help him, but Dustin's injuries were too serious. As a result of a punctured lung and severe brain trauma, he only lived a few minutes before dying in Kyle's arms.

Kyle was traumatized, as we all were, from the accident that took his friend's life. But it was Kyle's fate to be there with Dustin; to comfort him in his last moments before he passed away.

For me, it was a mother's worst nightmare come true. I remember wishing that Dave and Buck hadn't taken me to the hospital when they did, because if I had died, Dustin wouldn't have gone to work that week. He would have been at my funeral instead. It should have been my funeral, not his! He was only seventeen.

It would be years before I could cope with the tragic loss of my beautiful son. What made it worse is that I couldn't do anything about it, even though, I knew.

CHAPTER THREE

LEGENDS OF THE LOCK

B EAVER CREEK STATE PARK IS reputedly the largest haunted area in the state of Ohio. Sprucevale was a small town located within the park, and its former site is where many of the legends are concentrated. Once a thriving community, the town was abandoned in 1870 after the collapse of the Sandy and Beaver Canal. All that remains is a stone grist mill.

Dustin fell from a cliff directly above Beaver Creek in Sprucevale. There are many legends associated with this place, but the story of Gretchen's Lock is perhaps the most famous.

Gretchen's Lock

The legend of Gretchen's Lock is the story about a little girl named Gretchen Gill. She was an infant when she left Ireland with her family to come to the United States. Her father, Edward Gill, had been contracted to build the locks for the canal system.

Unfortunately, Gretchen's mother became very ill and passed away on the voyage to the United States. Gretchen and her father continued their journey and arrived in Sprucevale, Ohio in 1834, where he would build the Sandy Beaver Canal System.

Three years after their arrival, Gretchen contracted malaria. According to state park records, Gretchen cried out during her fevers and delusional spells that she wanted to join her mother, before passing away herself.

Grief-stricken at the loss of his daughter, Edward Gill submerged Gretchen's coffin in the waters of the lock, now known as Gretchen's Lock. When the canal failed in 1852, he left for Europe with Gretchen's remains. The ship was lost at sea and everyone aboard perished. Legend has it that every year, on the anniversary of Gretchen's death, she can be seen walking up the creek, crying, and looking for her mother.

Bride at the Bridge

The date was August 12, 1837. Esther Hale was a young woman who, like many her age, was excited about getting married. Flowers and vines decorated the parlor, and a wedding cake covered with cheesecloth was on the kitchen table.

She was dressed in a beautiful wedding gown anxiously awaiting her groom to arrive. He never came. Several hours went by before the guests and the minister finally left.

Esther sent someone to look for her groom at his cabin, but he wasn't there. She was filled with despair as she closed the curtains to block out the light. They were never opened again.

She walked the bridge every day for months looking for him. After no one had seen her for a while, her neighbors stopped by her cabin, only to find her decaying body still dressed in her wedding gown.

Legend has it that on the anniversary of the day she was to be married she appears as a hideous apparition. She walks on the bridge, still wearing her tattered wedding gown. It is also said that if you touch her, you will die and she will become young again.

The Mushroom Lady

Her name was Lucy Cobb, and she was the best cook in town. Lucy fell in love with a young man named Tommy. She took him food on a regular basis in an attempt to win his heart.

One day she brought his food to him and found him with another young lady. Tommy introduced her to Sarah and informed her that they were going to be married. Lucy was devastated.

After regaining her composure, Lucy invited the couple over for dinner. They graciously accepted and went to her home, never to be seen again.

The townspeople never looked for Tommy and Sarah because it was assumed that they had eloped. It wasn't until many years later that their bones were found buried in the garden behind Lucy's house.

Legend has it that the three of them still haunt Sprucevale to this day. Ghost hunting crews claim to have made contact with them through EVP readings and that electronic devices quit working when Lucy is around.

The Young Boy

A young boy hanged himself from the rafters in a house just inside the entrance to Gretchen's Lock. Not as much is known about what happened to him and why.

It is said that pictures taken of the house always had anomalies in them because the spirit of the boy did not want photographs to be taken at the place of his death.

The concrete slab is all that remains of the building now. It is said that if you place a penny on the concrete step, you can watch it move.

Jake's Lock

Jake's Lock is named after a former caretaker who was killed when he was struck by lightning while making his rounds. Legend has it that he can be seen on stormy nights standing on the lock with his lantern.

There are various versions of the different legends that can be looked up on line. Ohioexploration.com and the Carnegie Public Library, as well as a host of other sites specializing in the paranormal, are good resources if you are interested in learning more.

Gretchen's Lock and the surrounding Sprucevale area is a popular site for ghost hunters. Ghosting 12 offers tours there several times a year. The director of the organization is extremely knowledgeable with the history of the area, and she enjoys sharing her knowledge with others. It was on one of these tours I attended in 2010 that I was told why the area was so haunted.

When the white men first came to the Sprucevale area, they slaughtered all the Indians there. Their bodies were hung upside down in the trees that were once located at the entrance of what is now Gretchen's Lock. It was meant to be a warning to the other Indians to stay away.

This horrific act of savagery cursed the land, and is believed to be the reason the souls of those who die there are unable to pass over and are doomed to remain there forever.

The Vortex

Shortly after we lost our Dustin, I was told that there was a gateway to another dimension in the area where he fell. I was so grief stricken at the time that I didn't give it much thought.

Then, on Dustin's birthday in 2012, we got a picture at the cross that his friends had put up as a memorial, and it showed a vortex in the background. This is the photo that adorns the cover of this book. The beautiful, swirling colors are mesmerizing and seem to pull you in.

I wondered, could this be the gateway that I was told about? Or did I somehow jar the camera? I'd never had a picture turn out like that before, and the only thing I was sure about was that it was gorgeous. Either way, it is an amazing photo.

When I got close to finishing this book, I looked for a photo of Dustin that I could use in it. He and his friend had exchanged phones so they could take pictures of each other on the cliffs, so I looked on his phone. (And yes, we still keep it charged). I found half a dozen pictures of him standing against the steep, rocky hillside. He was grinning from ear to ear in every one.

Then I noticed one of the photos had a vortex on the cliff above where Dustin was standing; where the cross is now. It was taken just ninety minutes before he fell. This vortex is in the same place as the one in the picture I took three years later; just from a different perspective.

Dustin's Grandpa

A few days after the accident, we received a phone call from someone Dave knew. Neither of us can recall who it was but we'll never forget what they had to say. She said she had a friend who was a psychic, and that she had a message for us. Her friend frequented Gretchen's Lock so when she heard about Dustin, she went there to try to connect with him.

It was a hot summer day. She sat on a bench between the parking lot and the creek and stared across to the hill on the other side. Dustin had fallen a hundred feet from the cliffs above before landing on a rocky area about fifty feet up from the creek.

She closed her eyes and opened her mind to receive some incredible images. She saw Dustin walking toward her, joined by a small, elderly gentleman. He led Dustin to a brilliant light emanating from the heavens, and then they both disappeared.

Dustin's grandfather, who fit the description perfectly, had passed just ten months before. The news of this sighting was comforting. Dustin was with family who loved him, and it was a relief to know that he had not fallen prey to the curse that haunts the lock.

Lucy's Dream

Dustin had a friend named David who had a cousin that lived across the street from David's house. Her name was Lucy. She was a few years younger than they were and totally infatuated with Dustin. She liked to hang around when he visited David because Dustin always made her laugh. And you can imagine how cool this fifteen-year-old girl thought these two older guys were. After all, they were seventeen.

Lucy was extremely traumatized when Dustin passed because she had never experienced a loss like that before. Then, one night, she had a dream. She was with a friend and trying desperately to get her to go to Gretchen's Lock with her. Her friend just really didn't want to go, but Lucy was determined.

She made her own way to the Lock, although I'm not sure how because she didn't drive yet, but hey, it was a dream, so anything can happen.

Lucy was mesmerized as she watched the moonlight glisten on the water. She was startled when she saw a figure approaching her. When he got closer she recognized him—it was Dustin! But how could this be? He was gone, but there he was.

When Dustin reached her he wrapped his arms around her and hugged her tight. He softly whispered in her ear, "Tell everyone I am all right. Really, I am all right." As he pulled away from her, she could see that smile he was so famous for, and it gave her a sense of peace. He really was all right.

He gave her a wink and turned to look behind him. There was a little girl with him. She looked like she had been crying. Dustin smiled at Lucy as he took the hand of the little girl and led her to a bright light that was shining down from the heavens, and they disappeared.

When Lucy woke up, she was amazed and a little confused. Her heart was pounding because she had never had a dream like that before. It was so vivid and seemed so very real.

We all have a purpose—a reason for being. Dustin was a gift from God and blessed by the Angels. He proved himself worthy in seventeen short years, and God needed him for something big. Did Dustin die at Gretchen's Lock to help the lost souls there? Did he lead Gretchen home to her mother?

The legend continues.

CHAPTER FOUR

THE ORBS

A PICTURE TAKEN BY ONE of Dustin's friends at Gretchen's Lock shortly after the accident was posted on Facebook. Glistening rays of sunshine cascade down the trees that camouflage the steep cliffs along Beaver Creek. A glowing green orb of light appears to be shining through the foliage at the very spot where Dustin landed after falling from the cliff above. It was there that he took his last breath.

I wondered if the green glow could have been a photographic anomaly. I also considered the possibility that a rescue worker might have left a glow stick at the scene, but if that were true, it seems unlikely it would have been visible through all the foliage. It is doubtful we will ever know exactly what it was, but one thing is for sure; it was a sign of things to come.

A Memory Carved in Gold

Another picture of interest was posted on Facebook several months later by two of Dustin's classmates, Beth and Maddy. They were very close friends and had all participated in Track.

The picture shows them proudly displaying the pumpkins they had carved for Halloween in honor of their fallen friend, Dustin. Beth's had his initials, "DMH," and hearts, etched into it, while Maddy's had his track number, "102," with stars.

A bright orb of light can be seen on the outside of Beth's left thigh. It is opalescent white with a violet halo around it. This was the second strange ball of light we had seen in photos since we lost our Dustin. I was not clear about what it meant, but it was beautiful for sure.

Homecoming

It wasn't long before a third picture that had a similar glowing ball of light in it was posted on Facebook. It was taken at the 2009 Salem High School Homecoming Dance.

Dustin's good friend, Devon, is looking dapper in his suit and tie as he stands between two beautiful young ladies dressed in elegant gowns. He is smiling like the Cheshire Cat, with his arms wrapped around their shoulders.

The red wristband that Devon wears in memory of his friend is visible on his right wrist. It reads, "Huffman Legend—Run Fast." Sure enough, a bright, glowing orb is sitting right on top of the wristband. Dustin and Devon had double dated at the homecoming dance the previous year. Is it possible that he was literally there again in spirit?

Inspired

By now I had seen three pictures that had these mysterious balls of light in them, and my curiosity was getting the best of me. Could this be what Eden was talking about when she said that Dustin was sending me the orbs to let me know he was okay?

I also wondered if I could capture some of them in my photos, so I got my camera and went to Dustin's Cross. His friends built it for him out of treated 4X4s. It stands ten feet tall, and is located just a few yards from the cliff where he fell. This memorial serves as a tribute for the devotion they have for him, and many people continue to visit it today.

Orbs Galore

The pictures Dave and I took at Dustin's Cross produced many orbs. There were big ones and little ones. Most of them were white with a violet halo around them, but occasionally there were other colors—green, pink, orange and red, to name a few. Sometimes there were just one or two orbs in the photos, but occasionally there were hundreds of them that looked like stars twinkling in the sky.

The pictures we took down at the bottom of the cliff rarely ever produced any orbs. Dustin's Cross and the overlook were the only places that we were getting them.

We began to notice that the appearance of the orbs in our photos not only depended upon where they were taken, but when as well. Holidays and Dustin's birthdays always produced the most amazing photos, while at other times there weren't any at all.

I was very excited about this mysterious new phenomenon, but my husband did not share my enthusiasm at first. "No, I don't want to think that Dustin is stuck here," he argued. Dave wanted to believe that he was in Heaven and at peace.

I told my husband that I believed Heaven is in another dimension and that when your body dies it might be possible for your soul to travel back and forth. I don't know why I believed this; I just did, and always have.

Three different cameras, all of which we had owned for years before the accident, were now producing beautiful balls of light. We had never gotten them in our pictures before, so why now? It wasn't long before Dave, too, thought it possible that these orbs were somehow connected to Dustin.

Discussions about the orbs with friends inevitably followed and led to various reactions. Some people I knew were in awe, while others were just very skeptical.

One family member (who wishes to remain anonymous) was especially worried about me. We had many intense discussions about the orbs. She didn't doubt their existence, but she was fearful that their source might not be what I thought it was. Because of my great respect for her, she often left me doubting myself. Still, I could not help myself. I was obsessed with taking pictures now.

Dustin's Birthday

On August 21, 2010 we celebrated Dustin's nineteenth birthday. I invited family and friends over for a cookout because I was sure if we had a party for him that he would come. We sat around the fire and reminisced about days gone by, talking about how very much we missed our Dustin.

Before the night was over, I took out my camera and took lots of pictures, hoping that one might reveal a sign that Dustin was with us for his birthday party. Not only did I get a photo with what appeared to be a moving orb of light, but also the image of Dustin's face right next to it! I was right! It was Dustin.

I was ecstatic when I showed my proof to the previously mentioned family member. She couldn't deny it now. Or so I thought. To my dismay, she said, "It does look like Dustin, but it's the Devil trying to trick you. Heaven is such a wonderful place that no one would ever want to come back here."

I insisted that, unlike someone who was elderly and suffering from an aging body, Dustin was not ready to go when he did. He was young and healthy and having so much fun. And he loved his family and friends so much that I think he would want to check on us. He would have to know that we'd be having a hard time grieving for him. But as much as I wanted to believe I was right, she had me doubting myself again; but not enough to keep me from pursuing what I wanted to believe was real.

The Investigation

On October 24, 2010, Ghosting 12 came to my home. It is a group that does paranormal investigations. They had heard about all the orb photos I was getting, so they came and set up shop.

Quite a crowd joined us, including Dave's sister, Debbie, who brought a friend along. Debbie and I had both gone to school with Jennifer, but she moved out west shortly after graduation. She just happened to be in town visiting friends and family. Jennifer brought her high-end Olympus camera with her. She had been taking pictures with it for over three years and had never captured an orb before. Seventeen out of the twenty-seven pictures she took in my backyard that night had the mysterious balls of light in them.

Our neighbors, as well as many others who were there, had orbs in their photos as well. Some people came simply out of curiosity, even though they were skeptical, but everyone went home believers.

Holy Orb

On November 28, 2010 we had family over for a nice dinner at our house to celebrate Thanksgiving. I took lots of pictures, hoping that Dustin would show us his presence. After taking a few photos, I put the camera up and forgot about it. Months later, I came across it and downloaded the photos onto my computer.

One of photos looked like some sort of overexposure. I almost deleted it. There was a huge ball of light on the ground in front of the gazebo with another brilliant light beaming downward from the sky. A closer look revealed an image in the top of the huge ball of light on the ground. I zoomed in to see a face.

It looked like Jesus! Or at least what I imagined Jesus would look like. He was wearing a traditional robe and had dark, shoulder length hair with a scar on his right temple. A crop and overall highlight resulted in brilliant colors where the crown, throat and heart chakras would be.

A few weeks later, I watched a documentary on the Shroud of Turin on the History Channel. Because the Shroud is two dimensional, they explained, the image on it is distorted when laid out flat. Scientists used mathematical equations to construct a three-dimensional figure based on the image. The wounds on the figure they constructed mirror the Shroud's bloodstains, including a large one on the temple. The scientists' performed tests that confirmed: IF the Shroud of Turin was Jesus' burial cloth, then the three-dimensional figure they created would accurately represent what He would have looked like. The resemblance to the face in my orb is remarkable; right down to the scar on the right temple.

A picture of Jesus was painted by real life child prodigy artist, Akiane. She created her masterpiece, also known as *Prince of Peace*, at the age of eight years old, and claims that it was a result of Divine Guidance. It was presented on Glenn Beck's website, *The Blaze*, and also in the movie, *Heaven is For Real*. The similarity between her painting of Jesus, the scientists' rendition of the image from the Shroud, and the face in my photo is remarkable and beyond coincidence.

I was convinced the orbs were spiritually pure in nature now. The devil wouldn't send me a picture of Jesus.

One Sweet Orb

This next story is one of my favorites. Dustin started a sweet tradition years ago when he would walk into the house and reach into his pocket for a half-eaten bag of Peanut M&Ms. He would cock his head, with that big ornery grin on his face, and toss them to me. "Aww, thanks, Dude," was my typical reply. He knew I loved Peanut M&M's, but what I loved even more was that he was sweet enough to save half of his bag for me.

Since Dustin's passing, I always take a bag of Peanut M&Ms with me whenever I go to his cross. I walk over to the cliff where he fell and pour half of the bag into my hand. After a short prayer, I throw them over the cliff, yelling, "I love you, Dustin!" My husband took a picture of me while performing this ritual. The colorful candies can be seen suspended in midair with an orb that appears to be in motion going after them. Pretty sweet, don't you think? Pun intended.

It's a Sign

Shortly after the accident, a good friend of mine told me that her parents were part of an organization called Friends of the Park. They told her that the park director had discussed renaming the Sprucevale Overlook to The Dustin Huffman Memorial Overlook.

After the initial shock of the accident wore off, I recalled what she said and contacted Ranger Todd to inquire about it. He said he would do what he could to make it happen, but the state did not have funding for signage. I told Todd that we would gladly provide a sign for the overlook if it were renamed in Dustin's honor.

Finding a company to make the sign was much easier than coming up with the words to put on it. I wrote a few paragraphs and then rewrote them again and again. It had to be perfect. I was so indecisive about the final draft that I reached out to my friend and author, Catherine Ryan Hyde, who wrote the book *Pay It Forward*. The movie based on her book was one of Dustin's favorites, and I believe it greatly influenced his pay-it-forward-lifestyle. It was a great honor to have her help me, and we corresponded several times before finalizing the memorial.

DUSTIN HUFFMAN MEMORIAL OVERLOOK

Dustin Marshall Huffman lived his life with a "Pay It Forward" lifestyle, always there to help out, even if it was for a stranger. He was pure goodness, with a touch of orneriness, and a smile that could light up a room.

On June 30, 2009, Dustin lost his footing and tragically lost his life while working nearby for a local tree service. He had an old-fashioned work ethic and was an incredible athlete, winning a state championship in track just three weeks before. Revered as a great teammate, he put his heart into everything he did, often encouraging others to do the same. He will be forever remembered by all who knew him for his love of life and compassion for others.

The Dustin Huffman Memorial Scholarship was created to honor the memory of this incredible young man and is intended to encourage others to "Respect life, work hard, and help others as Dustin did."

The sign sits in front of a few tall oak trees, atop a steep cliff, with a beautiful view of Beaver Creek below. There is a pull-off, so it is a popular spot to stop and a favorite for local photographers. On clear nights, countless stars twinkle across the expansive sky.

In another picture taken by my husband, a brilliant glowing orb can be seen just a few feet above the sign. It has a tail like a comet, as if it is traveling at a great rate of speed. It seems Dustin was letting us know how proud he was of his memorial and still just as energetic in his after-life as he was when he was with us in the physical world.

Man's Best Friend

On another occasion, I took several consecutive pictures of my husband standing by Dustin's Cross. The ground was covered with snow, and the blue sky peeked through the trees. A single orb that appeared to be moving in toward him from the right was much closer to him in the second photo, with a smaller orb following it. The photos were amazing and gave credibility to the idea that they were in motion, traveling across the landscape.

I showed this picture to an Angel medium in Cleveland. Her name was Debbie Michaels and she founded the ministry Where Angels Gather. She was middle aged with long, dark hair, kind eyes, and a gentle demeanor.

We talked for a while, but it wasn't long before Debbie said,

"Your son is here. He is right beside you." She told me that he had volunteered to stay with me throughout my lifetime. Dave got emotional and told her that he felt slighted, but she informed him that he didn't need Dustin as much as I did.

When I showed her the picture with two orbs, I told her I was sure it was Dustin with his grandfather. He had passed away eight months earlier. Without any hesitation, she replied, "No, that's a dog." I questioned her because I was sure it was his grandfather. It was comforting to believe that he was with a family member who was looking out for him.

She insisted, "That's his dog."

I argued that Dustin's dog, Ginger, was still alive to which she replied, "I don't care. That is a dog. Dogs have souls too, you know."

We talked for a long time. She seemed to be very impressed with Dustin and said, "He is not an Angel, but he is the closest thing I have ever seen to one that wasn't." I left feeling quite elated, but somewhat confused about the dog that she said was present with him in the photos.

My mind was racing on the way home. Then I remembered! Someone told me that their dog passed at the same time as Dustin, but for the life of me, I could not remember who it was. Three days later, it hit me. It was Dustin's friend's dad, who told me about it. His name was Bud.

I'd became friends with Bud's wife, Lori, so I called her right away but she was working. I had to know and couldn't wait to hear back so I sent her daughter, Cassie, a text and asked, "Did your dog die around the same time that Dustin did?"

I was stunned when I got her reply, "Yes, our Maxie passed just forty-five minutes before Dustin."

Maxie was a big, lovable German Shepard who always wanted to be involved with whatever was going on at the time. They said Maxie loved everyone but had a very special bond with Dustin. He spent a lot of time at the Myers' home, and no matter who else was there, Maxie was always by his side. It appears that she still is.

Christmas at the Cross

Our second Christmas without our Dustin was as bad as the first, so we went to the cross early in the morning to pray. We had decorated a Christmas tree and attached it to the base of the cross. A wreath hung on the top, and a light dusting of snow sat on the ground around it.

A photo I took of Dave next to the cross shows a beautiful orb on the Christmas tree. If you zoom in on the orb, you can see that it has a face in it that appears to be three-dimensional, sort of like a dime. This is one of many orbs that are very similar to each other.

My husband took two consecutive photos of me standing next to Dustin's Cross. Miniature orbs appear to be moving upward on my snowsuit in both pictures. They were all over me. They were on my cheek and my chin on the first and on the tip of my nose in the second. I imagined these tiny light beings as fairies or nature angels; or maybe the smaller animals of the forest who had passed there. And I felt very privileged that they wanted to say hi.

My Angel

Another orb, more than three times bigger than the average one, has appeared with me in a number of photos. Patterns and images fill the opalescent ball, giving it an even more mysterious appearance.

This orb was on the center of my stomach in a picture taken at Dustin's Cross, and again above my head on a tree in my backyard, as well as a few others. I like to think this one is my Guardian Angel�֎

Guardians of the Vortex

Just inside the woods behind Dustin's Cross is the setting for one of the most unique and beautiful pictures of all. For me, it is bittersweet. There is a tree about halfway down the path, where the terrain slopes downward to the edge of the cliff where Dustin fell.

The scene is framed with another tree and beautiful green foliage. In addition to the opalescent white orb we typically see, there are a variety of distinctly different colored orbs present: red, orange, light green and pink. Once again Dustin's signature orb has a long tail, looking like a comet travelling through space, while all the other orbs are perfectly round and focused in the picture.

Our Shooting Star

Last but not least is a picture taken by my husband using his iPhone. An orb can be seen shooting right out of the center of Dustin's Cross. It leaves a trail of light several feet long and makes for an amazing photo.

Since our first orb sightings, there have been many more, each with their own unique signatures. I was told by a medium that the orb in the picture taken at the cliffs right after the accident was green because Dustin's soul was healing from the trauma and he was going through a period of transition.

We believe Dustin's Orb is the one with the image of his face next to it. Makes sense, right? It is also consistent with the orbs in other pictures, such as the one with the M&Ms and the one above the Dustin Huffman Memorial Overlook sign. Typically, this orb has a tail like a comet, giving it the appearance that it is in motion. Dustin always was in constant motion in life, and very fast. It makes perfect sense.

If it wasn't for Eden calling us to let us know that Dustin was sending the orbs, we may never have known to look for them.

CHAPTER FIVE

Image Courtesy of *The Salem News*

TRAVEL TALES

Dead Battery

DAVE REFUSED TO GO TO Gretchen's Lock with me, no matter how much I begged. It had been almost a year, but he still couldn't bring himself to go there. It was just too painful and stirred up visions of his son's tragic fate that he couldn't deal with. I was drawn to the place and felt compelled to go there, but I always had to find someone else to go with me.

One day, Dustin's girlfriend, Brooke, whom he had been in love with since seventh grade, agreed to tag along. After a forty-minute drive through the winding countryside, we arrived at our destination—Gretchen's Lock.

We pulled into the lot and parked the car across from the creek. The towering cliff on the other side is where Dustin fell. After a few minutes of complete silence, we got out of the car and walked over to the water. The tears flowed as we gave each other comfort.

When we got back in the car to leave, it wouldn't start. We hadn't left the lights on or played the radio, but the battery was dead nonetheless, and the car was not going to start. It ran fine on the way down to the park, and I had never had any trouble with the battery before.

My car was an Audi A4 with a triptronic shift option. Dustin loved his truck, but driving my car was fun since he could run through the gears manually. He would often borrow my car to go to the movies with his friends, since it would accommodate more passengers than his truck. Well, that and just because he thought it was so cool.

Now Brooke and I were stranded and needed Dave's help. I tried calling him, but there was no cell phone signal. I tried again and again, until finally I got through. It was difficult to talk to him with all the static, but he finally figured out what was going on. He had to come down now.

When Dave arrived he checked out the car, and sure enough the battery was completely dead. It had never died before, and he accused me of leaving the lights on or playing the radio. I defended myself, insisting I had done neither. The car started right away when he jumped the battery, and we didn't have any more trouble with it for over a year, when we finally replaced it.

Dave's first time at Gretchen's Lock was an emotional one, but he overcame his fear. After that, we started going there together on a regular basis. Could this have been Dustin's way of helping his dad?

No Brakes

On July 1st, 2010, the state of Ohio dedicated the Dustin Huffman Memorial Overlook. The event was going to be huge, with a picnic and music to follow. Dave took our camper down and parked it on a grassy area across from the cliffs. We thought it might be nice to have Dustin's Danger Ranger there (that's what he called his little red Ford Ranger). It has a large dent in the right front fender from when a tree jumped out in front of him. Ha Ha. Well, at least that was his story.

Since Dave had to haul the fifth-wheel down with his big truck, I had to drive Dustin's. I loved driving it because it brought back the memory of how excited Dustin was when we went to the dealership to get it.

The road going down into the park entrance is extremely winding and very steep. I had to press really hard to get the truck to slow down, but since I wasn't used to driving it I figured that it was the nature of those brakes.

It was difficult to slow the truck down, but I hugged the curves and made it to the entrance of the park and over to where we had parked the camper.

Dave and I both arrived about the same time and began to set up camp. We put the awning out and set up some tables to sell T-shirts for the Dustin Huffman Memorial Scholarship. When everything was almost ready, Dave left in Dustin's truck to go to the overlook and check out the sign. He didn't get very far before he parked it and walked back. He approached me and asked with great concern, "Hun, how did you drive this thing all the way down here without any brakes?"

I didn't know what to say, except that it hadn't been easy. Dave took his truck into town and purchased some brake fluid to put in Dustin's truck before taking it up the hill. It was a miracle that I didn't end up driving off a cliff, and I feel very blessed that I had an Angel watching over me, keeping me safe the whole time.

Airborne

The following winter, there was another incident that could have resulted in a serious accident, but somehow, someone or something kept me safe. I had gone to Austintown to a friend's house to pick up a puppy for my mother. My friend, Sharon, had two four-month old Bichon Frise puppies available, and I wanted to get one for my mom. The puppy on the Little Caesar's dog food commercial just melted my mother's heart, and on several occasions she sighed and said, "Oh I would love to have a puppy like that."

Janet, who was a mutual friend of ours, told me about the upcoming litter a month before they were born. I asked her to let Sharon know that I wanted one of the pups. A few weeks later, three pups were born, but only two survived.

Some time later, Sharon was going through her car when she found the pamphlet from Dustin's funeral. This was odd, considering she always kept her car immaculate, but it was tucked neatly away in the glove box. Finding the pamphlet reminded her of me and that I wanted one of the pups, so she gave me a call. She said they would be ready to adopt in about six weeks.

When the time came, I gave Sharon a call to find out when I could come up to get one of the pups. I was disappointed to find out that she had gotten so attached that she couldn't give them up. She was keeping them.

The pups were almost four months old when Sharon came across the pamphlet from Dustin's funeral again. It made her think of me and how much I had wanted one of the puppies for my mother. In the meantime, she had given into the fact that it was just too hard with four dogs. She worked full time and couldn't give them the attention they deserved, so she called to see if I was still interested.

I went to her home after she got off work that evening. She invited me in and offered me a glass of wine. The puppies were in the living room, so I walked over to the couch and sat down. Suddenly, and with no warning, one of the puppies jumped right into my lap. He was wiggling with excitement and licking me all over. He never got out of my lap the entire time I was there.

There was no decision to be made between the two pups. Peppi, as my mother would later call him, picked me. We visited for a little while, before I put him in a carrier and headed for home.

It was a typical February day in Ohio, which meant blizzard conditions and terrible roads. Snow banks were piled high from all the plowing over the long winter, and the ditches were filled with snow.

The puppy was in the carrier in the front seat, scared and crying. My heart was breaking for the poor little thing. He had just been taken from the only family and home he had ever known. I turned on the dash light and unzipped the top of the carrier.

I reached in to pet the little guy when I felt my car shaking and rumbling like crazy. There I was, in the ditch on a forty-five-degree angle, plowing through the snow. A veil of white sheared across the window, making it impossible to see.

I closed my eyes and held my breath as I clenched the steering wheel with all my might. "Oh my God, oh my God," I screamed. The rumbling stopped as the car went airborne, and for a few seconds I felt weightless, as if I were defying the law of gravity. I felt the jolt of the car hitting the asphalt, but then it landed in my lane and continued down the road as if nothing had happened. I was shaking like a stick, and my adrenaline was off the charts. It was just crazy, but the car didn't have a scratch on it.

Dustin was known for driving around in wintertime looking for people to pull out of ditches. Maybe it was just for fun, or maybe it was because it made him feel good to help people. Either way, he did it, and just maybe, he was there for me.

Another Dead Battery

I love driving Dustin's Red Ford Ranger, or as he jokingly called it, his Danger Ranger. It is the perfect truck for me and my camping adventures. The bed of the truck has plenty of room for my tent and gear, and the extended cab has just enough room for my Amelia, a seventy-five-pound Pit-Lab mix.

It was summer of 2016 when my friend Janet and I went camping on my property in Hocking County. We spent three nights and four days basking in nature. There's nothing like waking up in the morning to the sounds of birds chirping and going to sleep at night listening to the crickets and frogs. Hiking entertained us during the day while campfires were the highlight of the evenings. And Amelia was in her glory because she could run free.

The three-and-a-half-hour drive there is worth it, but the drive home always seems to take forever. It's just so hard to leave my sanctuary. It's God's country.

After dropping Janet off at her house, I was finally almost home. Fifteen minutes later, I was turning up the street to my house when I noticed the odometer. It read 102,102. A feeling of sentiment overcame me. Dustin's track number was 102, so this was very significant to me.

I pulled into the driveway and parked the truck. The trip was exhausting, but I forced myself to unload everything and put it away so I wouldn't have to deal with it later.

The next morning, my husband was going to run some errands. He wanted to take our car, but I had parked the truck behind it so he had to move it first. The problem was, it wouldn't start. The battery was dead, so he jumped it to get it going. He left it running while he moved the car, and then he put the truck in the garage on the charger.

A few hours later, he returned to check the voltage on the battery. It was still dead, so he charged it for a few more hours. When he checked it again, it was still dead, so he removed it and took it to the auto parts store to have it checked. They said it was so dead that it was no longer chargeable. This didn't make any sense. I hadn't had any trouble with it on my trip as I drove it one-hundred and eighty-five miles each way. The alternator should have charged it. The thing is, I made it home safe and sound with no problem. Was it luck, or was it Divine Intervention?

My car battery goes dead for no reason where Dustin passed away, I arrive safely where Dustin passed after driving his truck down steep hills with no brakes, I'm launched out of a ditch and back safely onto the road, I make it home with a dead battery after a long road trip—these are all things that have happened with no logical explanation. I believe my Dustin was there every time keeping me safe.

CHAPTER SIX

ELECTRONICALLY SPEAKING

The Empty Seat

IT WAS GRADUATION DAY FOR the Salem High School Class of 2010 and a somber one for Dave and me. We were to attend the ceremony to receive Dustin's honorary diploma on his behalf.

My husband and I both felt the same anxiety and sadness about going, but we had to do this. Dustin's classmates would all be there, and we needed to go for them. They had been there for us; many of them still came to see us on a regular basis.

We stopped at a local drug store on the way to the school to pick up some graduation cards. Dave waited in the car while I ran inside to get them. When I returned to the car, I found Dave in tears, just staring at his phone. He had just received an incoming call from an unknown number, and Dustin's picture appeared on the screen.

It only rang once, and Dave was trembling as he answered his phone, but there was only silence. He sobbed uncontrollably, and I was speechless for just a moment before I was brought to tears.

How could this happen? Pictures appear on incoming calls when a number is tagged with a photo, but this was an unknown number.

We took a few minutes to regain our composure and went to the graduation. The seats in the auditorium were filled with proud parents and other family members there to recognize and honor the accomplishments of their loved ones. There was an empty seat with a graduation cap on it where Dustin would have been seated. This was supposed to be a happy day, and he should have been there.

But maybe, just maybe, the empty seat wasn't empty after all.

Ghost Radar

I was desperate to communicate with my son after he passed away. Then one day I came across an app on my phone. It was called Ghost Radar, and out of curiosity I downloaded it. It was free, and what could it hurt?

I opened the app for the first time as I walked into Dustin's bedroom. It looked like a sonar screen where an incoming object would blip intermittently. Words appeared on the screen within seconds, one right after another: "Climb, Fell, Difficult, Breathe, Blood."

The vision of seeing him fall off the cliff, landing a hundred feet below and gasping for his last breath was horrifying. I broke down. My husband came running when he heard me sobbing and crying. He stared in disbelief when I held up my phone and showed him.

The words on the screen accurately described Dustin's fate to a T. He climbed the cliff and punctured his lung as a result of his fall, suffocating on his own blood. It was as if he was telling me exactly what happened to him. What are the odds of Ghost Radar producing these words in that sequence?

What happened later is another example of when Ghost Radar produced words that made us believe Dustin was communicating with us. He and his brother, Casey, planned to get their last name written vertically on the outside of their right calves. They would have to wait until Dustin turned eighteen, because there was no way I was going to allow it.

After Dustin passed, many of his friends got tattoos in his memory. Even the assistant principal of the high school has "HUFF" written on his right arm. It makes us proud that so many people honored his memory in this way

Casey went with Dave and me to get tattoos in Dustin's honor. I watched as everyone else got theirs, and I was up last. "I changed my mind. I don't want to do it," I whined. No way was I going to do it, but my husband pressured me to follow through with it. Dave and I both got the scholarship logo, which was created by my friend, Eska.

A few days after the accident, my friend, Eska, asked me if she could borrow Dustin's track shoes. I reluctantly gave them to her, letting her know she couldn't keep them long. They were very sentimental, and giving them up for even just a few days made me very anxious.

Eska suspended the shoes from her chandelier and took quite a few pictures, until she finally got the perfect one. Then she turned the photo into a graphic and added wings with the words "Dustin Huffman" arched above the shoes and "Memorial Scholarship" under the wings. It was the perfect logo for the scholarship that had been created to honor Dustin. There are at least three of Dustin's friends that got the same tattoo.

Casey got the "HUFFMAN" tattoo down his leg, just like he and Dustin had planned. Ghost radar later revealed the words, "Casey, Birth, Mark, Written, Happily." It seems pretty self-explanatory.

Then there was the time that Dave and I were playing with Ghost Radar and I jokingly said, "We should ask Dustin for a stock tip." Seconds later the words came: "Tip, Copper." Dave and I just looked at each other dumbfounded. Then we busted out laughing. We didn't take it seriously enough to actually invest any money, but out of curiosity I started following copper on the stock exchange. It turns out that copper had just bottomed out and it would have been a great time to buy it.

A few months later we joked about the stock market again, and within seconds the word came: "Copper." It had steadily increased in value since the day of the first tip and now it was going back down again a second time. Bottom line, if we had bought and sold when we got those messages, we'd have made a fortune.

The Race Is On

We had always gotten Dustin the latest and greatest techno gadgets, and he would have loved the iPad when it came out. It was just a little over a year after the accident when Dave purchased one for me. He was hoping that a new toy might be a good distraction and make me feel better because I was still so depressed. I remember thinking how excited Dustin would've been.

Dave downloaded a race game and played it a few times, but he spent most of his time on his computer. I used it daily to check my email and find out what was going on in Facebook. Every night I would close all the apps before putting it on my dresser to charge while I slept. This was my regular routine, and that night was no different.

When I woke up in the morning I remembered having had a rather unusual dream. Dustin was there, in my room, sitting on the end of my bed. There was no conversation between us, but simply the comforting sense of his presence. It was wonderful.

The next morning, I picked up my iPad off of the dresser, and I heard a rumbling noise coming from it. It seemed strange because that never happened before. When I opened it up, I saw the race car game in play.

I immediately went to Dave and asked him if he'd played it again after I went to bed. His eyes were wide with surprise when I showed it to him because he had not played it, but the Bentley Roadster was the car in play. Upgrades could only be achieved through high scores that unlocked better cars. The Bentley Roadster was the best car you could get, and Dave was still driving a Chevette or something like that.

Dave tried racing the Bentley in the game, but it was much too fast for him. It wasn't long before he crashed and burned, and he never came close to getting a fast car again. Funny coincidence—the Bentley Roadster also happened to be Dustin's dream car.

Was it just a dream, or was Dustin there that night? Was he playing the race game on our new iPad?

Many people believe that spirits can and do manipulate electronics as a means of communication. My own personal experiences validate this theory.

CHAPTER SEVEN

333

When you see
a 333
repeatedly

It's a sign
from the Divine
All will be fine

IN THE CARDS

W HEN I WAS A LITTLE girl, my mother told me that my grandmother used to get her tarot cards read on a regular basis. I always envisioned her sitting at a table with a little old lady in traditional gypsy attire. I personally had never had my cards read before, but the idea intrigued me.

In March of 2012, I went to a Journey Fair in Pittsburgh. The event is held annually, hosting a variety of vendors that make for a very interesting day. The two-day event was not far from where my dear, sweet Aunt Helen lived, so I made arrangements to stay with her overnight.

We used to spend a week with her and my cousins every summer when we were kids, and she was my favorite aunt. My father would get so mad at us kids when it was time to leave because he could never find us. We would either be hiding in the woods or down by the creek. It worked out great that the Journey Fair was so close to her.

There were a lot of psychic mediums, so of course I had to get several readings. An ionic foot bath detox was interesting and disgusting all at the same time. I also purchased some essential oils, of which a Chai Roll-On has become my favorite and a staple that I keep on hand at all times. It not only smells wonderful, but it is very calming and works well with my Reiki treatments.

And I can't forget the rocks. There were so many cool rocks, and I came really close to leaving with a beautiful cathedral purple amethyst geode. I now regret not buying it, because it turns out that it would have been a great deal.

Doreen Virtue gave an interesting presentation on Angels at the expo. She had a variety of books for sale through Hay House Publishing, so I purchased one for her to sign afterwards.

I started receiving promotional emails from Hay House, but I certainly didn't mind. There were so many interesting books, and this is where I found the oracle cards.

There were a variety of cards by different people, but I was most interested in Doreen Virtue's Angel Cards. After all, if they provided messages from Angels, they couldn't be bad. She had a wide selection to choose from, and after some thought, I ordered the *Archangel Oracle Cards*.

The cards came in the mail within a few days, and I was more than a little nervous as I opened them up. I read the book and followed the directions on consecrating the deck. First you hold the deck in one hand, and using your knuckles on your other, you firmly wrap the deck to release any energies connected to it. Then you touch each card, one by one, imprinting the deck with your own energetic signature. Finally, you fan the deck out widely over your chest with the intention of radiating positive energy from your heart into the cards.

My signature shuffle incorporates the number 333 because it has always been my special number. I was born on the ninth day of the year, which is three plus three plus three, at exactly 3:33 AM. Many nights I have awoken suddenly only to look at my clock to see that it was 3:33 AM.

A perfect example of the number 333 showing up right when I needed it was when I was on a retreat in Sedona, Arizona. The group of girls I was with wanted me to go on a helicopter ride over the Grand Canyon. The very idea made my knees weak and gave me butterflies in my stomach. No way was I going to do it, but they pleaded with me. They said that they needed one more person, or none of them would be able to go.

Reluctantly I agreed, but I wasn't very happy about it. All the anxiety that I had been experiencing dissipated immediately when we approached the helicopter and marked on the side of it in big, bold numbers was "333." It turned out to be an amazing experience, one that I will never forget or regret.

Another example where the number 333 helped to guide me was when I was on my way to the airport to go to the Speak, Write, Promote Conference in Orlando, Florida. I had received an email from Hay House Publishing about it, and it was just what I needed to boost my writing career and increase the chances of my book becoming a success. The problem was, I wasn't sure I could justify spending that much money on myself. For weeks, I anguished over whether or not I should go. At the last minute, I got out my credit card and signed up.

Soon my bags were packed and my husband and I were on our way to the airport. We were both hungry, so we stopped at a McDonald's on our way there. The line for the drive-thru was long, with cars backed up around the corner, so I went inside. There were several people in front of me, so I waited patiently for my turn.

I was preoccupied with my trip and off in my own little world wondering if I should really be doing this. When it was my turn, I gave my order to the server and she rang it up. She placed the receipt on the counter to be attached to the bag once the order was filled. I looked down at it to see in bold print the number 333. A smile came over my face with the confirmation that I was most definitely on the right path.

Gentleness

The cards were ready for their first reading, and I was actually a little scared. I shuffled the cards using the technique known as the riffle, or dovetail, shuffle. With half of the deck in each hand and my thumbs inward, I released the cards while lifting them, causing a bridge that put the cards back into place. I did this three times and then proceeded with the overhand shuffle. I grasped a group of cards and cut them into the deck in three sections, doing this a total of three times. This way I was able to incorporate 333 into my shuffling.

I proceeded with my reading and turned over the card "Gentleness," and then checked the guide that came with the deck for its meaning. The guide is meant to be used in conjunction with what your intuition tells you. I had been through something traumatic, and I needed to take the time to be gentle with myself so that I could heal. It made perfect sense.

I put the cards away after this initial reading and didn't get them back out until the next morning. Still a little nervous, I shuffled them with my personalized 333-technique and turned over a card. It was "Gentleness" again. Keep in mind that there is only one card of each kind in a deck of fifty-six cards, so the odds of getting the same one twice in a row were extremely low.

That evening I thought, "I'm going to try this again," so I got out my deck of cards and shuffled. When the "Gentleness" card came up again, I couldn't believe my eyes! It was way beyond a coincidence now. The odds of coming up with the same card three times in a row were nearly statistically impossible. I interpreted this as a sign that I did not have anything to fear and that I could trust the cards.

Dragonflies

My friend, Lisa, gave me another deck of cards as a gift when I was at a retreat in Sedona, Arizona, that she hosted in October of 2012. It was the *Earth Magic Oracle Cards Deck*, by Steven D. Farmer.

I shuffled the deck for the first time with my 333 technique and turned over the card "Dragonfly." After consulting the guide and using my intuition to interpret the card, it was clear. It represented Emergence: I was evolving.

The following day I got the cards out and did a second reading. It was a pleasant surprise when once again the card "Dragonfly" turned up, this time being followed by the "River" card.

Later that day, Lisa took us to Montezuma's Well, which is a natural limestone sinkhole where 1,500,000 gallons of water emerge daily from an underground spring. The inhabitants of the area built a canal around 700 BC to irrigate their crops.

The natives that used to reside there considered this water to be sacred and healing, so I splashed some onto a rash that I had on my chin. My doctor had prescribed various creams over the past six months, none of which worked to rid me of this embarrassing red rash. The water from Montezuma's Well was truly healing. Within one day the rash was completely gone!

When it was time to go, we followed the path along the canal back up to the rim of the well. About halfway back, I noticed two dragonflies on the ground next to the canal. One was hyacinth blue and the other was crimson red. It seemed as though the dragonfly theme was going to continue in my life for a while.

Adjacent to the canal that flowed alongside the well was a creek. Ironically, it was named Beaver Creek. The same name as the creek in Ohio where my son lost his life. It was amazing that the cards I drew that morning were Dragonfly and River, and now here I was at Beaver Creek in Arizona with two beautiful dragonflies.

The following day I went shopping with some of the girls in my group. I have never been much for a lot of jewelry, but they wanted to go into a local jewelry store, so I tagged along and proceeded to browse. It wasn't long before a beautiful rose coral dragonfly necklace and pair of earrings caught my eye. The dragonfly necklace was calling me, and I had to have the earrings.

It is said that signs appear in threes, and once again, the number three has made itself known to me in three pairs. First the dragonfly showed up in the cards twice. Next I saw a pair of beautiful dragonflies between Montezuma's Well and Beaver Creek. Then I found a dragonfly necklace and matching earrings. This is synchronicity at its finest.

The symbolic meaning of the dragonfly is emergence, or the transformation of one's self. If you're in this period, it is one of heightened awareness, and it is best to surrender yourself to the flow of the Universe. It was an affirmation that I was on the right path; the path toward enlightenment.

The "River" card supports the dragonfly in several ways. In nature, water is symbolic of the subconscious mind, and we must be mindful when our deeper thoughts surface. The ancient Greeks observed that water transformed from liquid to solid to vapor, which symbolizes a metamorphosis, as does the dragonfly.

Drawing the Dragonfly and River card together told me that going with the flow and embracing these changes were what was meant to be. Just as the dragonfly emerges from the dark waters, I was entering the light, leaving the darkness behind.

Blue Butterflies

Lisa and I were talking on the phone one day, when all of a sudden she said, "I wondered when he was going to connect with me." I asked what she was talking about and she told me that Dustin had just shown up.

My heart was filled with joy at the very thought of him being there. The rush of excitement was exhilarating, and I was consumed with anticipation.

After letting me know what Dustin had to say, Lisa finished by telling me that Dustin wanted me to know he would be sending me blue butterflies. I was a little disappointed, because I had never seen a blue butterfly here in Ohio—except for those in a conservatory—and I doubted that I would see one now.

A few weeks later, Lisa came to my house for a meditation class in my backyard. I looked over at her and said, "No blue butterflies yet." She just shrugged her shoulders and smiled.

This was also the same day that Dustin's friend, Gary, had a terrible car accident and he was in bad shape. I told everyone about it, so after the class, we all sat on the ground in a circle and held hands to say a prayer for him. After several minutes, I opened my eyes to see a small, pale blue butterfly on Gary's picture that we had placed on the ground in the center of our circle. "Lisa, look!" I exclaimed. Once again she gave me a big smile and nodded, looking happy and feeling validated about her message.

About a week later, I was outside with my mother sitting in the swing in front of my water garden, when I saw a big, beautiful black and blue butterfly land in front of me. It was stunning.

I had told Gary's mom about the blue butterfly on his picture when we had the prayer for him. When Tori and Ben took Gary home from the hospital a few weeks later, they found a beautiful blue butterfly in their yard next to the house. She sent me a picture of it and said, "I can't believe my eyes. I've never seen one like that before, and it is just keeps hanging around." Since the sightings of the beautiful blue butterflies in 2011, I have seen them every year.

In December of 2013, I purchased the *Talking to Heaven* oracle cards by Doreen Virtue and James Van Praagh. My first card was, "I send you loving signs through nature," and it had a picture of a beautiful butterfly.

CHAPTER EIGHT

SONGS FROM HEAVEN

I BELIEVE THAT THE MUSICAL greats of our time and times past were divinely guided to create their exquisite masterpieces. From the most famous classical composers to down-home country music artists, they tune into the Source and pull from the universal knowledge, arranging melodies and writing words of wisdom to enlighten the world.

I had just such an experience when I was nineteen years old. I couldn't sleep, so I crept quietly into the living room and snuggled down onto the couch. The light from the lamp post shone into the living room through the bay window, and the plants on the windowsill made for a beautiful border. It was so very tranquil.

I closed my eyes and started to drift off when I could hear the faint sound of the most beautiful and gentle Angelic music I had ever heard. As I focused my attention to tune into it, the volume seemed to get louder and louder, to the point that, just for a second, I worried it was going to wake my mom and dad. Then I thought for a moment and realized that only I could hear it.

I stared up at the ceiling in a trance-like state, when suddenly, fluorescent butterflies materialized in all of the colors of the rainbow and began dancing an elegant ballet to the mesmerizing music. I laid there for a while, watching these beautiful beings frolic to and fro with the utmost grace, before finally falling asleep. It was the most spiritual experience I have ever had in my life.

In 2011 at the Journey Expo, I purchased a CD by Doreen Virtue, which was divinely guided music from the Angels. There was something familiar about it. I would put it on and go to sleep listening to it several nights a week, and I still do to this day because it is so relaxing.

One day I had a revelation and remembered where I had heard this music before. It was the same music I'd heard in the living room when I was gifted with the beautiful Butterfly Ballet.

I have heard the same music again on a number of occasions. The first few times it happened, I had to check my phone to see if my music app was on, but it never was. Twice I was standing in front of the kitchen sink, looking out at the backyard, and on several other occasions I heard it while looking out the window of my room at The International Center for Meditation, on Heavenly Mountain in North Carolina.

I truly believe that I was visited by Angels in my living room that night and that they spoke to me through their beautiful melodies. And I'm sure that they still come back occasionally to remind me who I am.

I saw a friend's post on Facebook talking about having a similar experience. Comments from her other friends revealed that they also hear the music, so it is more common than I originally thought. If you open your mind to it, you just might hear it too.

I Won't Let Go

I had been off work for over two years since Dustin's accident, and although I wasn't with it mentally or emotionally yet, finances deemed it necessary for me to find a job. My experience and accounting background made it fairly easy to secure employment, but actually going to work proved to be more difficult.

Getting ready was a real chore. Crying made it extremely difficult to put on makeup, and I had to give up wearing mascara altogether. The grief of losing my son seemed unbearable, and I often cried as

I left for work, making the drive tedious as it was difficult to see through all the tears.

One day was particularly hard. I was sobbing uncontrollably as I drove up the street, and I needed a distraction. I turned the stereo on my favorite country station to hear the songs that Dustin loved so much. This was always a source of comfort. The song "I Won't Let Go," by Rascal Flatts, was playing.

> It hurts my heart
> To see you cry.
> I know it's dark,
> This part of life.

The words in this song resonated with my heart. It was as if Dustin were talking to me.

The song is about someone who is going through a difficult time and feeling very lost. It assures you that you are not alone and that they will help you through this terrible time. It talks of drying your tears and holding you tight. The words could not have been more perfect.

The next day I got into my car to go to work, once again with tear-filled eyes. After backing out of the drive, I headed up the street and turned the radio on. The song, "I Won't Let Go" was playing again!

The third day that I had to work that week was no different, and I left the house an emotional basket case. Once again I turned on the radio as I drove up the street, and once again I heard the words, "I won't let go." Signs come in threes, and this happened three times in a row that week. I thought it was Dustin comforting me. For me, there was no other explanation. It would be much later when I realized that I was wrong about it.

Take A Back Road

A few weeks had gone by when I drove Dustin's truck to transport some water plants that I was picking up from a friend after work. I drove to Dawn's home in Canton, where she had started a lovely tea house, elegantly decorated with a beautiful water garden. She'd had the water garden for a while, so the plants needed thinning and she was happy to share them with me.

After our visit, I programmed my GPS and headed home. Dawn lived in a suburb off the beaten path, and I'd have probably gotten lost otherwise. My GPS was programed to take me on main highways, but for some reason I found myself out in the country on back roads that day. I was out in the middle of nowhere and had to turn the radio off to silence the annoying static.

It was a beautiful spring day, with crisp clean air. New foliage spread out on the trees, and plants of a vivid green and flowers of bright colors were in full bloom. The gravel road had twists and turns, and a little one-lane bridge crossed over a creek in a wooded area, where two small fawns stopped to get a drink.

It was amazing, and I was filled with gratitude for such an experience. "Look, Dustin, check that out," I exclaimed. I talked to him as if he was right there, especially since I happened to be driving his truck. I left the passenger seat clear just for him, although I'm sure he'd have preferred to be the one driving his truck. Ha Ha!

The drive seemed magical, and I was not a bit worried about the unfamiliar territory. Soon enough, I began to recognize landmarks as I got closer to home, and I figured the radio might work, so I reached down to turn it on. The song "Take a Back Road," by Rodney Atkins, was playing.

> And it makes me wanna take a back road.
> Makes me wanna take the long way home.
> Put a little gravel in my travel,
> Unwind, unravel all night long

I just knew that this was Dustin's way of letting me know he was with me.

It was six months later, in January of 2011, when I went to Sedona, Arizona for Reiki Training at the Infinite Light Healing Studies. There I met a psychic named Baker.

We sat down to talk and she asked if I had any questions for Dustin. Of course I had many, but the first thing that came to mind was if he sent me songs.

Baker asked what song, and when I told her "I Won't Let Go," she closed her eyes and went into a trance-like state. She opened her eyes a few moments later to say, "No. He knows you want to believe that he sent it, but he didn't. Are there any others?"

I was surprised to say the least, because I was sure he'd sent me that song to comfort me in my time of need. "Okay then, how about 'Take A Back Road'?" I replied.

Once again she closed her eyes. After a short pause she began smiling and then opened them to say, "Yes, he thought that was pretty funny." That would be so like him. He always was on the ornery side.

I wasn't just sure now that he had somehow played that song for me, I was also convinced that he manipulated my GPS to deter me from the highway to the backroads. My GPS had always taken me down highways before, and on that trip I had even crossed Route 62, which goes straight through my hometown.

When We All Get To Heaven

After I got home from Arizona, I went to Dustin's Cross. I said a prayer and performed my tradition of throwing the M&Ms over the cliff before getting back into my car. It was a bitter cold day in February, but I didn't care. I rolled the windows down to play our song and blasted the stereo, singing along to "Take A Back Road."

When it was over, I manually selected the song "I Won't Let Go" and said aloud, "I know she said you didn't send me this song, but I want to believe you did, so I'm gonna play it anyways."

The song was almost over when I felt like something hit me in my chest. It just about knocked the wind out of me. It was a revelation! I knew at that moment that Dustin didn't send me that song— Jesus did! Seconds later the next song, "When We All Get to Heaven," by Brad Paisley, began to play.

> Sing the wondrous love of Jesus.
> Sing his mercy and his grace.
> In the mansions bright and blessed,
> He'll prepare for us a place.

My music was set on shuffle, and out of the hundreds of songs on my iPhone, this one came within seconds after my epiphany. Thank you, Jesus.

CHAPTER NINE

ASK AND YE SHALL RECEIVE

The Bobby Pin

S EVERAL MONTHS AFTER THE ACCIDENT, my mother and I went to the cemetery and parked in our usual spot. A huge oak tree, majestic with its leaves in full fall colors, provided some shade where we parked. Dustin is buried next to my brother, Marshall. Mom was vigilant about taking care of his grave, and now it was my responsibility to take care of Dustin's.

We went there to plant crocus bulbs, envisioning how beautiful it would be to have these colorful little flowers blooming in the springtime. We gathered up our supplies and walked down the hill to where our two boys were laid to rest. The cemetery was deserted except for us, and it was eerily quiet.

I made a grid with string so that all the rows would evenly cover the grave. It hadn't occurred to me that it might be a good idea to have my hair up when planting. It kept falling in my face as I leaned over to dig the holes for the bulbs.

I was quite annoyed at having to constantly flip my hair out of my face, and I finally blurted out in frustration, "God, it would have been a good idea if I had put my hair up." No sooner did I get the words out of my mouth than I spotted a large bobby pin between the blades of grass close to where I was digging. Seriously, I couldn't have found it if I was looking for it! And it was exactly like the hairpins that I always use to put my hair up in a French Twist.

"Mom, look!" I exclaimed.

She hadn't been paying attention to me, as she was preoccupied with her own thoughts, and she didn't quite understand what I was trying to tell her, so I explained it again. She just smiled and we finished planting.

I'm not sure my mother understood what I was trying to tell her, but that was okay because it was meant for me.

Decorating by Storm

It would be our first Christmas without Dustin, and I wanted to decorate his cross at Beaver Creek. Dave still couldn't bring himself to go to there, but I was drawn to this place. My husband told Dustin's sister, Mandy, that he would stay with her girls if she would go with me. I gathered up the decorations and we were on our way.

It was an unusually warm afternoon with severe storms throughout the county. The sky was dark with huge black clouds, except for when lightning bolts lit up the sky. Thunder roared and reverberated across the land.

It probably wasn't the best time to go, but there were only a few days before Christmas, and this was something I had to do. I would never forgive myself if I didn't get his cross decorated, and not even Mother Nature was going to stop me.

We were almost there when we encountered the Sheriff redirecting traffic. He told us that we had to turn back because a huge tree had fallen across the roadway. He also said that trees and power lines were down all over the county.

Mandy and I were even more anxious now because neither of us knew an alternate route to Dustin's Cross, but going home was not an option. We followed our instincts and turned onto a road that wound up, down and around through the hilly terrain. Somehow we managed to find our way to Dustin's Cross.

When we arrived, we noticed a small circle of blue sky directly above us. We were literally standing under the only part of the sky, as far as I could see, that wasn't storming. Time was of the essence, so we got busy.

We used wire to attach a small Christmas tree to the base of the cross and decorated it with solar powered lights. Wristbands inscribed with "Huffman Legend...Run Fast" were folded in half and tied together with a wire hook to look like little red bows. We put dozens of them on the tree and then added white snowflake ornaments.

Then it started to rain. In my frustration I threw my arms up and yelled toward the heavens, "We're not done yet!" The rain stopped immediately. I looked to the heavens and smiled and said, "Thank you."

To finish it off, we began wrapping rocks with multi-colored foil to look like presents and placed them under the tree. When we were done we got into the car, and it immediately started to torrentially downpour. The rain pounded the windshield with such force it made it difficult to see, and hail bounced off the car in every direction. The drive home was slow and tedious, but we made it safe and sound.

Since then, we have had similar experiences. Dustin's friends host an annual picnic at Gretchen's Lock to remember him. On one occasion, it had been raining all day, but Dustin's friends still gathered at Gretchen's Lock to remember him. They had no sooner gotten there when the dark clouds disappeared, allowing the sunshine to illuminate the sky and warm the earth.

The same thing happened to my family when we went down on a picnic the following year. It rained everywhere else around us, but it was as if we were in a protective bubble.

Dustin's friend, Nate, told us that he went to the cemetery after working out one day. He didn't care that it was pouring down rain. He was going to sit with his friend. He pulled into the cemetery and parked his car, and the rain just stopped.

In each of the previous scenarios, the rain started again when it was time to leave.

Catherine's Angel

It was a nice day. The weather was warm, which was always appreciated after a long cold winter in Ohio. I was driving up the street toward my house when I noticed a sale going on at one of my neighbor's.

"Damn," I thought as I drove by, remembering that I had missed the estate sale for my good friend's mother the week before. Marsha told me about it, and I wanted to go, but it had slipped my mind. I remember feeling really bad about missing it because Marsha's mother and I shared a very special bond. Not that I was her favorite as a teenager because Marsha and I had been pretty ornery and gotten in a lot of trouble together in our younger years. It was later, when I lost my Dustin, that her heart broke for me as she also knew the devastating grief from losing a child. She lost her son over 40 years before. It was a loss that she never got over.

I continued down the street a few hundred yards but then turned around. For some reason I felt the need to go back to my neighbor's sale. I parked on the street and walked up to the house. The driveway and garage were filled with tables displaying various items for sale. A large, beautiful lighted deer caught my eye, but Christmas was a long time away, and it would just be one more thing to store, so I decided not to get it. I certainly didn't need more stuff. If anything, I needed to have my own sale. So what was I even doing there?

I wandered around and found myself in a different area, where I was greeted by Mickey. She was handling the sale. "Hello, are you looking for anything in particular," she asked.

"Not really," I replied. After thinking about it for a minute, I asked, "Do you happen to have any crystals or Angels?"

Mickey looked at me in disbelief and responded by saying, "I do. I have an exquisite Angel necklace made of pewter and crystal that didn't sell from an estate sale we held last weekend." We exchanged phone numbers and she promised to get back with me after checking with the family to see if they still had it.

A few days went by before she called me to say that she could stop by my house and drop the necklace off anytime. I told her how excited I was about it, and a few hours later she brought it over. She told me that she really didn't understand why it didn't sell because it was so very unique and beautiful. It turns out that it had belonged to Marsha's mother, Catherine. It was her favorite necklace, and she always wore it to church. It was then that we realized the reason it hadn't sold before. It was meant for me.

The Raffle

The Inaugural RUN FAST WINGED 5K was held on August 22, 2015 to benefit the Dustin Huffman Memorial Scholarship. The event was a huge success. There was an exceptional turnout, in part because of the media coverage. The television news crew showed up early to interview the volunteers for the *WFMJ Today* show. They also highlighted the raffle baskets that were beautifully displayed on three long tables. There were many baskets, from detailing supplies donated by AutoZone to high end cosmetics from Dillard's Department Store.

I was putting the baskets together when I noticed there were two gift certificates for the Dawgy Pawlor, a dog groomer in my hometown. They were each valued at forty-five dollars, so I couldn't decide if I should do them separate or together. Even winning just one would be a good score.

Then I thought how I had been wanting to get my Sam groomed. He was a Border Collie Mix and shed so much that I had to sweep every day. Getting his thick undercoat professionally brushed out always helped immensely, but funds were tight, and there just wasn't enough extra money for it. Then I had a selfish thought. I could raffle one of them and keep the other. I even said aloud, "You know, one of these would be enough to be put out, and I could keep the other for Sam."

And then I thought, no, I can't do that. They were both donated for the raffle, and it just wouldn't be right. As much as I would have loved to keep one, I put them both on the table as separate raffles. That was the right thing to do. I took a deep sigh and moved on to finishing the rest of the baskets.

People started showing up to register for the race. After getting their t-shirts, most people headed over to the raffle baskets. They were a big hit. People love raffle baskets! I wanted to get some tickets myself, but I had forgotten my money, so I asked my mom if I could borrow ten dollars. That was enough to get fifteen tickets, so I put one to two tickets in the bags for each of my favorite baskets.

Soon enough it was time for the 5K. It was amazing and wonderful that the 2015 recipient of the Dustin Huffman Memorial Scholarship actually won the race. Zach Morris won the scholarship award based on his honor and integrity, only to turn around and win the 5K.

After all the medals were awarded to the runners who placed in the race, it was time for the drawings. First we drew the winning ticket for the 50/50. The lucky winner was gracious enough to donate their winnings back to scholarship.

Next up was the drawing for the raffle baskets. There were quite a few so it took a while to get through them all. Finally, the gift certificate for the Dawgy Pawlor was drawn and to my surprise, my name was called. "Wow! I can't believe it. I actually won", I exclaimed. I was still carrying on about winning the gift certificate that I had wanted when I heard my name called again for the second Dawgy Pawlor gift certificate. Maybe karma rewarded me for doing the right thing. I could have kept one, but I didn't, and I ended up with both of them.

E2

In January of 2013, I bought Pam Grout's *New York Times* bestselling book *E2*. The book has experiments at the end of each chapter meant for you to complete. They prove reality is malleable and that you shape it with your mind.

The first experiment is referred to as "The Dude Abides" It requires you to choose something to ask for as a sign. It has to be something big; something that means a lot.

Six months earlier, I had lost an earring from a pair that Dustin had given me as a gift. They were my favorite, and I hadn't taken them off since the accident. Retracing my steps and looking for hours proved to be a waste of time, and I literally mourned for weeks. It felt like losing him all over again. Getting my earring back would be the perfect sign.

Now that my sign was picked, it was time to make the demand, and it went like this: "Dude, you know there is a lot of controversy down here about your existence. Would it hurt for you to give me a sign? And not just any sign. I want my earring back, and I want it in forty-eight hours." It made me a bit uncomfortable to make such a demand because a part of me was scared that I was going to be disappointed, and did I really dare talk to God that way? But I did it, and now it was time to wait and see.

The rest of the day was nothing out of the ordinary, and I remember praying that night asking God to please honor my request, apologizing for the manner in which it was made. The next morning, I went into the bathroom to wash my face and brush my teeth when I noticed that the stopper in the sink had been pulled up so it could drain better. It had gotten clogged from all the hair that had become entangled around it. It was more than a little gross, and the thought of brushing my teeth while having to look at this disgusting sight made me want to gag. I got a toothpick and pulled out the hair in the front of the drain. Then I leaned in to work on the back side of the plunger when I saw a glimmer of gold mixed in with the hair. I used the toothpick to pull it out, and lo and behold, it was my missing earring! I was ecstatic and ran to my husband with the news. God had answered my prayer and gave me back my precious gift from Dustin.

I got my earring back after it had been missing for over six months! Finding it at all was amazing. Finding it in less than twenty-four hours after telling God I wanted it back as a sign was a miracle!

As the saying goes, "Ask and ye shall receive."

CHAPTER TEN

WE'RE BACK

WE'D PRACTICALLY LIVED AT TIMASHAMIE Family Campground every spring, summer and fall for five years. There is a large club house at the entrance with a beautiful Olympic-size swimming pool. Large hardwoods frame its elongated figure-eight-shaped lake with an arched wooden bridge across the center. Campers surround the lake, with another row across the road along the Mahoning River.

The campground appears to be abandoned during the week, with the exception of the snowbirds who make Timashamie their home for the summer before returning south to escape the frigid temperatures in Ohio. It's peaceful, with soothing sounds of nature all around—the sound of the rustling creek, birds singing their melodies by day and frogs croaking their mating calls by night.

Weekends and holidays are always busy. Campers from all over come to get away from the hustle and bustle of their daily lives. They cruise up and down the road in their golf carts, going from one camper to the next, visiting family and friends. There are cookouts during the day and campfires at night.

Our first camper was an older twenty-two foot Layton given to me by my younger brother, Marshall. He had been living in it at another local campground, but he'd moved back home with our parents when he could no longer work and take care of himself. His debilitating depression broke the hearts of those of us who knew and loved him. Despite having a beautiful and devoted wife with two very gifted children, he just couldn't snap out of his illness.

As he grew more and more depressed, Marshall's successful career as a registered nurse came to an end. He had always been a body builder, very health conscious, and had never abused drugs or alcohol of any kind. Now a broken man, he was severely over-medicated with prescription drugs that numbed his brain and dulled his senses. We prayed that he would get better and encouraged him to stay with us whenever he wanted. Eventually he became so agoraphobic that he rarely ever left our parent's house.

The last time Marshall came to Timashamie was for a Holiday cookout, on April 20th, 2003. We were amazed at how good he was doing. I have a picture from that day, of him with Dustin on a paddle boat. They were both smiling from ear to ear.

It was wonderful to be able to celebrate Easter with my family there. I was lucky to still have my parents and both of my brothers with me. A picture taken that day of the five of us sitting together would be our last family photo.

On May 23rd, just four weeks later, my baby brother hung himself in the basement of our parent's home. My mother and father were destroyed, and the rest of us were devastated and in shock. Dustin was affected greatly by his uncle's suicide because the two of them were very close. This horrible tragedy would contribute to his outlook on life, as represented by the following paper he wrote just seven months before the accident that would take his own life.

LIFE

At only the age of seventeen I have had two major impacts on my life that I feel have made me grow into the young adult I am today. The impacts were two deaths in my close family. My grandfather and my uncle.

My grandfather had the best work ethic I had ever seen of or heard of. When my dad was growing up, my grandfather worked three jobs to keep my father and aunt healthy. Since his death, I have completely changed my outlook on life. I now work two jobs seven days a week and never complain or show bad emotions toward it. I try every day to be as good-hearted and as strong willed as my grandfather used to be.

The hard work and determination my grandfather had has also made me strive to be a better student. I will work hard, whether I end up successful or not, until the day I die because that's what my grandfather did and that's what my father wishes he could do for his family now. So I am going to make my family proud by being the best man I can be, every day. I will do this every day, because life is too short not to do it every day.

Life doesn't last long enough. Life is too short to be and stay unhappy. My uncle, at the age of forty-one, killed himself, and because of his death, I will never let myself hurt for a long period. Live life to learn and forget but remember the good times and the mistakes you did make to look back on what you have already handled and accomplished.

My life has been a good, strong life, but because of my family and their strength and will, the rest of my life will be the absolute best it could ever be. I miss my uncle and grandfather dearly, but I will always have them with me to keep me strong and determined, and that is why this is, My Life.

by Dustin Huffman   December 2008

We have Marshall to thank for our Timashamie days because we would have never looked into finding a campground had he not given us his camper. There was an open lot on the east end of Timashamie Lake. It was the perfect site, and the view was spectacular. Hues of orange and red reflected across the water from the setting sun, creating a mirrored image of the sky.

The front of the camper had cushioned seating on both sides, with a long table in between where we enjoyed our meals and played games. This area transformed into a king-size bed at night, so there was always room to have a slumber party. The kitchen and bathroom were not fancy, but they were adequate enough for our needs at the time.

We made a makeshift deck out of pallets that we covered with thick sheets of plywood and placed a little white picket fence around. It wasn't big, and it wasn't fancy, but we just loved our little place on the lake and how it opened up a whole new way of life for us.

Three years later, we moved to a site along the river when we bought a larger camper that could accommodate our growing needs. It was a thirty-eight-foot Dutchman camper with a large awning that spanned across a massive deck where we could enjoy the outdoors. The pool was visible between the two campers directly across the road, so I often used binoculars to check on Dustin when he was swimming.

The new camper had a master bedroom in the front for Dave and me and a bunk room in the back. The bunk room had bunk beds on one side and a booth that also converted into a bed on the other, so it could easily accommodate four kids. It was nice because they could play cards or watch TV in the evening in their own room.

I have so many great memories of Timashamie. We had family and friends out for cookouts, and at night we would sit around the fire, mesmerized by the dancing flames. And of course, the kids always loved roasting marshmallows to make s'mores. Dustin had the time of his life there, swimming, fishing, wading in the creek and exploring the countryside.

But, as the saying goes, "All good things must come to an end." Dustin and I were at the camper one night in late August of 2004. A torrential downpour that lasted for two days had dumped more than seven inches of rain on the area. Wind gusts of fifty miles an hour and large hail made it extremely dangerous to be outside.

The heavy rains and high winds made me nervous, so I called my husband to ask him what I should do. Dave reassured me that everything would be fine, but I decided to pack it in and go home anyways. My intuition proved to be right.

The lake and the river at the campground swelled and overflowed. The two were connected with water five feet high where the road once had been. The violent floodwaters tossed the campers around like dominoes, casting several of them into the swollen river. The raging flood battered the structures, leaving one camper several hundred feet downstream, torn into two. Debris littered the banks of the river for over a mile.

Our over-sized deck kept our camper in place, but it couldn't protect the interior. Water poured inside, filling the ductwork and electrical outlets, leaving behind a muddy mess before receding. The damage resulted in a total loss.

The campground suffered over five hundred thousand dollars in damages. It was a flood of epic proportion for the area, and the governor declared Columbiana County to be in a state of emergency.

After the storm we purchased a new camper with the insurance money. It was a two bedroom fifth wheel that was very similar to the camper we had lost, but we didn't go back to Timashamie except for a few short visits. Instead we tried out several different campgrounds, but it just wasn't the same.

Dustin begged us to go back to Timashamie, even into his teenage years, but it no longer seemed feasible. We had moved to a really great neighborhood, where there were lots of kids, and it was just one street over from his grandparents.

He made trails in the woods next door, where he loved to ride his dirt bike. There was a fire pit in the backyard where he spent a lot of time hanging out with friends when the weather permitted. When he wasn't outside, he was in the basement which we had remodeled to include a 42-inch plasma TV and a pool table. It was a great place for a kid.

Our camper sat in our side yard for several years without getting much use because none of the new campgrounds had worked out and life had gotten so busy. A few weeks after Dustin finished his junior year, he asked us if he could take it to Lakeside Campground on Berlin Lake. He and his friend, Nate, had met a couple of girls from a nearby town who camped there, and they were more than a little interested in them.

Dustin and Nate helped my husband work on the camper to get it ready for their adventure. The lot was reserved at Lakeside, and they were all set to go for the next weekend. Sadly, they did not get to go on their trip because Dustin would fall from the cliffs that would take his life just four days before the excursion they had planned.

Our friend, Bob, called to invite Dave and I camping a few weeks after Dustin's accident. We had several mutual friends who went to a music festival in Ithaca, New York every year. Bob encouraged my husband and myself to go because he thought it would be good for us to get away. He called repeatedly, insisting we go. We were like lost sheep, so it didn't take a whole lot of convincing before we gave in.

It was a last-minute decision, but we hooked our camper up to the truck and we were on our way. The camper didn't need any preparation since we'd had it ready for Dustin to use for the camping trip he was supposed to go on. It makes one wonder just how much of a coincidence that was.

The drive to Ithaca was going to take five and a half hours. We were almost half-way there when two guys in another truck passed us on the left. I looked over to see the passenger give us an obscene hand gesture.

"Oh my God, Hun. That guy just flipped us off!", I exclaimed in surprise.

A few minutes later, we were cruising along when I happened to notice something in the driver's side mirror. The siding was peeling off the camper and blowing in the wind. We pulled off to the side of the road to check it out and found that some pieces had actually blown off.

The mystery was solved as we figured that was why the two guys who passed us were so insolent. They may have, unintentionally, gotten assaulted by a flying piece of debris. You would think that they could have informed us of what was going on. We had no idea!

We waited on the side of the road for a while when Bob showed up to rescue us. Dave and I were not equipped to deal with this disaster. Bob had some duct tape and used it to secure the loose pieces of siding, and soon we were on our way again.

We arrived at the campground late that evening to find our friends with their campers set up in a field, arranged in a big circle. They didn't know we were coming, so we just parked across the way from them. We already knew some of the people in the group there, and they introduced us to their other friends.

While it was a great music festival, it was just too soon for us. We spent much of the time in our camper grieving. The following year we tried it again, but the memories from the first time made it unbearable, so it was our last time.

Four years passed since we had last used the camper, and finances were getting tight. I had not worked much after the accident. The price of diesel fuel to pull the camper with Dave's truck made it too expensive to take it anywhere, and we were paying insurance on something we weren't using. It didn't make sense to keep the camper any longer. Plus, I was tired of seeing it sitting in our side yard. I went to Timashamie Family Campground to see about getting a lot to put it on, thinking it might be easy to sell there.

It was a fifteen-minute drive, winding down and around through the hills on a back country road, to get to the campground. It was a drive I was all too familiar with. It just wasn't the same without Dustin.

I pulled into the campground to see that the clubhouse had a fresh coat of paint. The spring-fed lake had a new bridge across the center and was even more beautiful than before. The playground equipment had been replaced with new and improved models, and the Olympic-size swimming pool looked inviting. It was so beautiful, and my mind was flooded with memories from the past.

I was promptly greeted by the new owner, Vicky. It was a pleasant reunion, since we had known each other from another campground that we had tried out. I told her why I was there and asked about the availability of lots.

Vicky told me there were only two lots available on the outer row. All the local campgrounds were pretty much full up with workers needing housing, since the big oil boom had happened in the area.

"Seriously, there aren't any creek-side or lakeside lots at all?" I asked, somewhat dismayed.

She replied, "Well, there is one lot along the creek that became available last night, but we like to offer the premium sites to our current campers first, in case they want to move." That seemed fair, and I told her I understood but asked if I could see the lot anyways, in case no one else wanted it.

When Vicky told me it was lot number ninety-five, I lost it. I could not hold back the tears—it was our old lot! She had to give it to us, and there was no selling the camper now.

Dustin tried so many times to get us to go back to Timashamie. He finally got his way. We went back and spent three more wonderful years there. It was a place to reconnect with the past, find peace with the present, and reflect on the future.

CHAPTER ELEVEN

MI' PATH

Reiki by Mi'

M Y HUSBAND HAD BEEN GETTING cluster headaches for nine years. These headaches have been nicknamed suicide headaches, because many people have actually ended their own life to get relief from the excruciating pain. The headaches would come on suddenly and disappear just as quickly, rather than gradually subsiding. Watering eyes, nausea, and nasal congestion were common, and Dave spent many nights in the bathroom, vomiting because of the agonizing pain.

Oddly enough, Dave's headaches were seasonal. He would start getting them in January and they would last until April. He would get an eight-month reprieve, but the four months in which he had the headaches were almost unbearable.

With each passing year, the repeated attacks of excruciating pain intensified and became more and more debilitating. During these periods, Dave experienced symptoms of sleep deprivation because the headaches would wake him repeatedly through the night, making it impossible for him to go through the normal sleep cycles. They were affecting him mentally, emotionally and physically.

MRIs and a barrage of other tests were performed over the years, but doctors could not identify any specific cause. Oxygen therapy did provide some relief for a while. When Dave got a headache, he would put the mask on and breathe the pure oxygen for three to five minutes, and the pain would subside. As time went on, this became less and less effective, while the headaches became more and more frequent.

It was March of 2011, and we were both sleep deprived. The situation had become desperate, and I was at my wits' end, when

I called my friend, Bob. He was a massage therapist, and I was hoping he knew some technique that could help Dave. He said, "Michelle, I don't think there is anything that I can do, but I know this lady." He then told me that her name was Lou, and that she did Reiki.

I'd never heard of it before so I asked, "Reiki? What is that?" He said he didn't know exactly how it worked, but that it just did. He gave us her number so we could schedule an appointment. I had no idea just how much Reiki was going to change my life.

"Reiki is a Japanese technique for stress reduction and relaxation that also promotes healing." That is the official definition, as given by the International Center for Reiki Training. Reiki assists you in reaching a state that enhances the body's ability to heal itself. I have come to learn that it is exactly that and more. Reiki not only helps with healing our physical bodies, but also our mental and spiritual self. Caring for the Mind, Body, and Soul has long been a recognized practice in Eastern philosophies.

Dave went for several treatments before the headaches started to subside. They became less frequent and less severe, but they were still a serious problem for him.

In addition to dealing with Dave and his headaches, I was still dealing with the grief from losing Dustin. It had been over a year now and had only gotten worse, so I started seeing Lou for treatments, too.

Working with Lou was amazing, but it wasn't long before it became much too expensive for both of us, so I quit going. Still, I was intrigued with this mysterious healing energy, and I wanted to learn more. I found a Reiki Master Teacher named Lana on-line. On April 18th, 2011, I travelled to North Olmstead Falls to see her.

Lana was a retired psychologist and an amazing woman. We spent hours talking, and she demonstrated various techniques as well as attuning me to the Reiki frequencies. The experience transformed my emotionally fragile state into one of tranquility and peace. I imagined that this was how a monk must feel, as I walked around in a state of Zen with a gentle smile on my face. My hands were clasped together in prayer, thumbs pressed against my heart. I could feel the steady rhythm of my heartbeat. Nothing could phase me.

A few days after my attunement into Reiki, my husband and my son, Michael, came to me with a crisis—one of such magnitude that it would have previously sent me into a state of pure panic, since I seemed unable to handle stressful situations before. Now, instead of going into flip-out mode, I just smiled and said, "It will be fine." Dave and Michael both looked at me in disbelief and was like, "Who are you?" However, I'm pretty sure they did not want the old, stressed-out me to come back. Ha Ha.

After becoming a Reiki practitioner, I could work on Dave right away when he got his headaches, no matter what time of the day or night it was. This worked out much better than having to call and wait for an appointment. The first time I gave him a treatment was quite an experience for me. I said my prayer and placed my hands over his head. It was only a few minutes before his headache was completely gone, however, I experienced a headache the very moment his disappeared. I was shocked and surprised, to say the least. I very rarely ever get a headache—and it hurt! I was new to Reiki and didn't quite have all the techniques down yet.

The next time I worked on Dave, his headache went away again, but my sinuses started to pour. This was a typical symptom he would often experience when his headaches would subside but this time it happened to me instead.

Something was wrong. A Reiki practitioner shouldn't be adversely affected after giving someone a treatment, so I talked to a friend about it. She just smiled and said, "You forgot to ground yourself." I can tell you that I wasn't ever going to forget to do that again, and I have since learned how not to take on the symptoms of whomever I happen to be working on.

The good news is that after nine long years that Dave had to endure these debilitating headaches, it was over. In just a little over a month of regular Reiki treatments, Dave was free. He hasn't had a headache since.

Lisa taught me Reiki II several months later. I loved Lana, but besides being a little too far away, I wanted to experience the teachings and attunements from different teachers.

Several months later I received a phone call on the same day I was having a meditation class in my back yard. It was about Dustin's friend, Gary. He had been in a car accident and was hurt badly. They had to stabilize him from a punctured lung before they could operate on his broken back.

When Gary woke up after his surgery, he opened his eyes to see his mother standing beside him. He looked at her and said, "Mom, Huff was in the car with me when I was having my accident." Gary always called Dustin Huff. He was still heavily sedated and slipped back into a state of unconsciousness. When he woke up again he didn't remember anything about the accident or telling his mother that Dustin had been with him.

The doctors told Gary he would be in the hospital for four to six weeks, with a three percent chance of ever walking again—and that would be only after a year of physical therapy. This would not be good for anyone, let alone an extremely active twenty-year-old country boy, so we were all pretty scared.

I went to the hospital and gave him Reiki the day of the accident, and continued administering it every other day until he got out. He walked out of the hospital in nine days! Everyone, including the hospital staff, was shocked at how fast he had recovered from such serious injuries.

Two weeks later Gary stopped to see Dave and me after mowing his grandparents' lawn. I told him how lucky he was, but that he might be pushing it a bit. A few months later he got a job on the Ohio River loading cargo, and yes, he really did push it then. He had to go back in for another surgery, but he has since fully recovered.

A few months later, my father was diagnosed with a brain aneurism. The doctor at the Cleveland Clinic was very concerned because of how old he was, and recommended an angio-procedure. They would go into the femoral artery with specialized instruments and travel through to the site of the aneurism to block it off. The doctor said that was the best choice because it was non-invasive, and eighty-four-year-old diabetics do not typically heal well from brain surgery.

We went to the clinic for the procedure, but unfortunately it was a failure. The doctor said that he encountered too many obstacles just before reaching the affected area, preventing him from completing the procedure. We were all very upset because we had to schedule the dreaded brain surgery. It was my father's only option now.

Three weeks later, my father ventured out of the house for the first time since the failed angio procedure. He came to my place with my mom, and it was obvious he was not bouncing back well. It took a lot for him just to walk from his car to the house. His head hung low with a glazed look in his eyes as if no one was home. We worried that if this was what the "easy procedure" did to him, the brain surgery in two weeks might be more than he could handle.

My father did not believe in Reiki, and quite frankly, he thought that I had lost my mind. He thought that the death of my son had pushed me over the edge. It was understood in our family that we never brought such things up out of respect for him. He didn't need to get upset, especially with an inch-and-a-half brain aneurism that could burst at any time.

But when I saw him in that condition it broke my heart, and I just couldn't hold back anymore. I burst out, "Damn it, Dad. Just let me try. I promise, if you don't like it, I will never bring it up again. Please, just let me try." He was weak enough that he let me bully him onto my Reiki table.

"Are we done yet? Are we done yet?" was all I heard for twenty minutes, but we did get a mini treatment in. He went into the kitchen to wait for my mom while I worked on her. She and I both smiled when we heard him whistling away like a canary. He was very talented, in that he could whistle like a variety of songbirds.

My mother's face lit up as she said, "You know, I haven't heard him whistle in a long time."

The following day my father woke up energized for the first time in a long time. He told my mother that he wanted to go shopping at Sam's Club in Boardman, so they did just that. A few days later my father, the skeptic, came to me and asked, "Would you do that again?" And so I did, and I did it again every few days until the brain surgery.

He would always have more energy the day after getting a Reiki Treatment, so whenever I would work on him I would jokingly tell my mom to get ready to go shopping. And that's what they did, every time.

The dreaded day came when we had to go to Cleveland. It was a long drive in the wee hours of the morning. I never liked driving in the dark, whether it's morning or night. My night vision isn't the greatest, but we made it. My father was admitted as soon as we got there, and I got a room with my mom at the guesthouse.

It would be a while before they got the pre-surgery testing done, but we still didn't waste any time getting back to the hospital. When we got there we were directed to a room in pre-op. I had time to give him some last minute Reiki before they came in and took him.

The surgery was a success, and we were relieved when he regained consciousness in the recovery room. He was smiling from ear to ear, his head all wrapped in gauze, and said he was just really happy he woke up. He also told me that Dustin had been with him the whole time.

According to the doctor, a typical stay in the hospital for major brain surgery for someone of my dad's age and condition would be five to seven days. My father had brain surgery on Tuesday and was home on Thursday, and on a treadmill in two weeks.

The doctor was amazed with his recovery and said to him, "You are resilient." And then the doctor looked over at me, adding, "And maybe a little Reiki." He had previously dismissed it when I spoke to him about it at an earlier appointment.

The incision healed completely in six weeks, leaving little evidence of a scar. My father has since made a full recovery and tells everybody, "My daughter does Reiki."

My appetite for knowledge was insatiable at this point, so I began researching Reiki on-line. I found a Reiki Master-Teacher classes at the Peace Center in Sedona Arizona. The course was expensive, and combined with the airfare and lodging it seemed unaffordable, but my husband encouraged me to go, so I signed up on-line and made my travel arrangements.

Later that day, I was driving down the street when I noticed a bumper sticker on the car in front of me. It read, "COEXIST," with the words being created using various religious symbols. "WOW," I thought. "How cool is that! I wonder where I can get one of those?"

The following day I went to Boardman to look for a pair of boots for my trip, since I wanted to go hiking in the beautiful red rocks of Sedona. On my way there I saw another car in front of me with the same "COEXIST'" bumper sticker. I'd never seen these before, and now I'd seen two of them, two days in a row.

Once I got to Gabriel's Department Store, I went straight to the shoe department. To my surprise, there was only one pair of hiking boots and they were my size.

The time came for my trip, and I was on my way. After the long flight, I had to take a two-hour shuttle ride from Phoenix to Sedona. When I arrived, I went to the hotel just up the street from where my classes would be and checked in. It had been a long day, so I settled in for the night.

The next morning, I walked over to the Peace Center to sign in. I walked up to the counter when I noticed a stack of "COEXIST" bumper stickers. I knew then that this was where I was supposed to be.

The Reiki path has been a blessing and may very well have saved my life. It has given me a purpose and a sense of peace to be able to help others through spiritual means. It is a gift that we are all inherently endowed with. It is all a matter of remembering who we are and being open to it.

There were many skeptics around me that refused to believe in something that couldn't be scientifically proven, while others had religious convictions that weren't compatible with Reiki. One day my sister-in-law and I had a passionate discussion about this, which left me very worried afterwards that I might be doing something wrong.

That night I downloaded an audio Bible app on my iPhone and said a prayer asking God to please send me a sign. I needed to know I was doing the right thing.

Matthew 1:1 seemed like it would be a good place to start, so I turned it on and laid my head down on the pillow. I listened to it for a while before dozing off. In the morning I woke up and was disappointed because I didn't think I got my answer. I still didn't know what to do.

The Bible app had turned off at some point during the night, so I picked up my phone and looked to see where it ended, and here is what I read:

Matthew 10:1 "And Jesus called unto his disciples and gave them powers to cast out unclean spirits and heal all manner of sickness and disease." AMEN.

Yoga & Meditation

Yoga is a physical, mental, and spiritual practice which originated in India. It was not originally designed as an exercise in itself, but rather a technique to prepare the body for meditation. It centers and balances you, which can help you more easily deal with the trials and tribulations that life throws at you.

My husband had gone to the emergency room for chest pains and they kept him overnight as a precaution even though all the tests came back fine. The official diagnosis ended up being a panic attack.

The following day I was home having my own panic attack. It was almost noon and would soon be time for his discharge. I needed to get to the hospital, but I was emotionally, mentally and physically exhausted. I needed to get dressed, but all I could do was pace throughout the house wringing my hands.

It occurred to me that doing yoga might make me feel better, so I turned on the TV and started the DVD. At first each position took a lot of effort to do, and I had to force myself. It was exhausting, but I stayed with it. Following the yoga, I did the ten-minute meditation.

After that, I sat up on the floor with my legs crossed and hands together in prayer. Finally, I bowed my head, and with eyes closed, I saw a deep blue sea, which appeared to be fluid and deep, with flecks of sparkling pink and purple.

A jolt of energy burst through me and brought me to my feet. I felt amazing and was dressed and out the door in record time.

If I was a disciplined person, which I am not, I would practice yoga, every day, which I don't. I know I should, especially since my past experiences with it was so amazing and I know how good it makes me feel. This is an area in which I need to work on myself, however, I do meditate daily.

I met my friend, Eden, at a prayer class in the spring of 2011. She teaches meditation at her studio, Just Be Meditation, in Akron. We were both in Cleveland preparing to become ordained ministers with the fellowship, Where Angels Gather.

Eden is a beautiful soul, with long blonde hair, blue eyes, and a slender frame. When the class was over, she approached me and said, "You know, your son is always with you." Just the thought made me light up like a Christmas tree. She kept looking by my right shoulder and then said, "My, he has a lot of energy!"

I answered her with, "Yes, he always did."

With that she replied, "Oh honey, he still does." Then she shook her head and said, "And he's a little cocky." After hesitating, she added, "In a loving way." Yep, for sure. That would be him.

We only talked for a short while because we both had long drives home. I later regretted not getting her number because I wanted so very much to talk to this woman that could see Dustin beside me. Several months later, I bumped into her at a Journey Expo in Pittsburgh. I made sure to get her information, and we soon became friends. I asked if she would teach a class in Salem. A group of us would gather on Sundays in my back yard, where she would guide us into a state of total Zen.

My practice also includes listening to guided meditations. At first I would listen to them two to three times a day to be able to maintain a sense of peace, but now I only need to do it once a day. If I happen to miss several days in a row, I get out of sorts before I realize what is missing.

My favorite meditations are by Glenn Harrold, who is a renowned hypnotherapist from the United Kingdom. I have almost twenty of his apps on my iPhone. They are also available on MP3 download and CD, and while they aren't free, they are so very worth it and much cheaper than medication, without adverse side effects.

The meditations last between twenty to thirty-five minutes, and they take you through magical forests and waterfalls that cleanse your mind. Being too busy is not a good excuse to not do them, because they actually help to increase productivity, so it is a worthwhile investment of your time. These meditations leave you calm and centered, while at the same time being rested and invigorated. I have heard it said that a twenty-minute meditation is equal to a four-hour nap.

In an attempt to further my studies in the pursuit of enlightenment, I went to The International Center for Meditation in North Carolina. It hosts The Art of Living Institute, where a variety of classes and retreats are held. I took The Art of Living class my first time there and returned the following year to take The Art of Meditation. I hope to return someday soon to take The Art of Silence. They also have Yoga retreats and an amazing spa.

Studies have shown that meditation can help to regulate emotion. My husband says that it has made me a kinder, more gentle person and the sense of peace I have achieved supports this hypothesis. The Dalai Lama says, "If every eight-year-old is taught meditation, we will eliminate violence from the world within one generation.

The benefits of meditation can greatly improve the quality of one's life. Many illnesses are the result of stress and anyone who has lost a loved one knows the enormous stress that can be as a result of grieving.

Meditation also improves concentration. This is beneficial whether you are a student studying for a degree or a worker doing manual labor and everything in between. Simply put, improved concentration will help you perform better.

It encourages a healthy lifestyle, increases self-awareness, increases happiness, increases acceptance, benefits cardio-vascular and immune health, and slows down the aging process.

Actively participating in a meditation practice is a win-win. It has given me a much higher quality life than I could have ever had without it.

Apples and Chalkdust

It was years before I was able to go back to work, and even then it was difficult. Staring back and forth from paperwork to a computer monitor was painstakingly tedious and very hard on the eyes. It left me mentally exhausted, and I needed something different now.

After working several part-time accounting jobs, I found employment at the local golf club as a banquet server. It was great being able to do something physical and interact with people. The work was invigorating.

The flexibility was a big plus too. Instead of giving me a schedule, the banquet manager would text or call me to see if I was available. I could work if I wanted to, or not.

It was in October of 2016 when I ran into Betty at the golf club. It was a baby shower for her daughter. She had been a teacher at Salem High School for many years and knew Dustin well. Betty seemed surprised to see me and asked, "What are you doing working here?"

I laughed and replied, "I'm still trying to figure out what I want to do when I grow up."

Then she asked, "You have a degree, don't you?" and after acknowledging that I did, she continued by saying, "You should become a substitute teacher. We really need substitutes badly." I smiled at her and said I would think about it, but to be truthful, I never had any intention of pursuing it.

I worked as a substitute teacher a few times when I lived in Louisiana, but it didn't work out for me then. At that time I was still very young and lacked experience with children. I couldn't keep the kids in their seats, so I only did it a few times.

Many years later I was asked to substitute teach at Real Life Christian Academy. We sent Dustin there for first through third grades, so I taught his class on several occasions. I'll never forget how happy and proud he was that his mommy was his teacher. I only taught for a short time before getting a full-time job in accounting, which is what I really wanted to do and what I had gone to school for.

A few months had gone by since I'd talked to Betty at the banquet when I found a book on the picnic table in my back porch. It was titled, "Apples & Chalkdust" by Vicki Caruana and was a compilation of inspirational stories for teachers. Neither my husband nor myself had any idea where it could have come from. It was just the two of us now and we didn't get a lot of company, so it was almost as if it had materialized out of thin air.

I randomly opened the book near the middle of it and started reading. The passage at the beginning of the page read, "If there be any truer measure of a man than by what he does, it must be by what he gives." – Robert South.

A story about a new teacher on her first day followed. She was nervous and unsure that she would fit in. It wasn't long before the other teachers quickly welcomed her.

Finding this book and reading the story about a new teacher who was as nervous and scared as I was about venturing into a new career was inspiring. The universe was trying to tell me something. I was being guided to pursue this new path.

The next day I sent an email to the Salem City School district and inquired about the requirements to become a substitute school teacher. The class I needed to take was just a few weeks away and the following one wasn't until the next August, so I had to act quickly.

After taking the class at the Educational Service Center, the people there assisted me with the Ohio Department of Education's application process. A week later, I was awarded my Short Term Substitute General Education License.

Now for the scary part; it was time to go to work. I attended a meeting at the educational service center, where I signed up with the North Coast Shared Service Alliance. It was comprised of five different school districts in the county. The mediator told those of us in attendance that our information would be entered into the system the next day and that we could go to work as early as the following Monday.

The weekend seemed to take forever, and I was filled with apprehension about the new venture I was about to start. Monday morning came, and I anxiously waited for my first assignment. It was almost noon when the phone rang. The lady on the phone sounded a little desperate when she asked if I was available and if I could be there within the hour. I told her that I could be and, with a tone of relief in her voice, she thanked me before hanging up.

I got ready and headed out the door. The job was for an elementary school in a nearby town. It was a half an hour drive to the school, so there was plenty of time to worry about what my day would be like. Would the staff like me? Would the kids like me? And more importantly, would I be any good at this job?

Once I got there, I located the office, where I was greeted by the principal. We were both very surprised to see each other.

"Kim," I said, a little uncertainty in my voice.

"Yes," she replied. "I thought I recognized your name, but I wasn't sure if it was you or not."

I met Kim when we went to the music festival in Ithaca, New York just a few weeks after Dustin had passed away. She showed me where to sign in and directed me to the classroom. It was a fourth-grade class with about 25 students in it. They were all very sweet and treated me with the utmost respect. It was a good day.

I taught the elementary grades every day that week. Preschool and Kindergarten were my favorites. I loved the little ones and always took Dustin's favorite book to read to them. It was *The Grasshopper and The Ants*, and I used to read it to him all the time when he was little. The moral of the story is to work hard to prepare for your future, and I'm pretty sure this contributed, at least in part, to his incredible work ethic.

I love teaching at elementary schools. My favorite memory has to be when I taught art to a class of fourth graders. At the end of the day, a little boy brought me the picture he had drawn. It was a beautiful portrayal of a dandelion seed head.

The little boy melted my heart when he said so clearly and slowly in the soberest tone, "I want you to have this so that every time you look at it, you can remember this moment." Words cannot describe how this touched my soul. Yes, teaching was giving me exactly what I needed, and I was doing my best to give them what they needed, too.

I was packing up to leave for home on Friday afternoon after teaching a preschool class when I got a notice on my phone about an assignment at a middle school. It was great being with the little ones, but I wasn't too sure about the older kids. It was intimidating to say the least, so I did not accept it and went on my way.

When I got home, I attempted to check the website for substitute jobs to see if the assignment was still available, but I could not log on. My sign on was my phone number and my pin was the same as my phone, so it should be simple.

After repeated attempts that ended in failure, I resorted to the password reset. The email I received had me totally dumfounded. My user ID had mysteriously been changed to the phone number for the Dustin Huffman Memorial Scholarship. I would never have used that number for my sub account. Even more strange was that when I logged in, I was assigned the middle school assignment that I was so reluctant to take. It would have been easy to call in and cancel the job, but it seemed that this is what I was supposed to do.

The class went well, and I continued to take assignments for middle school as well as high school in communities other than Salem. I like to introduce students to my Tibetan singing bowl if time allows. It is usually well received and promotes a good rapport between us.

One day, I was offered a half day sub job at Salem High School. Anxiety consumed me because I wasn't sure I could handle it. Going to Dustin's school was difficult emotionally. Still, I accepted the job. I had to try.

Walking the halls of Salem Senior High School was very emotional.

This was Dustin's school, and I looked for him at every turn. I climbed the stairs to the second floor, where I saw Betty standing outside her class room. I stopped to say hello and told her how hard it was to be there. She smiled and reminded me that this is where he was loved so very much.

I found my way down the hall to my room and waited. Soon, the students came in and found their seats. I stood before the class to introduce myself and broke into tears. I was very embarrassed but the kindness and compassion that these kids showed me gave me the courage to continue on with my day.

A few weeks later, I accepted another assignment for Salem High School. As rough as the first one was, I needed to do it. This assignment was for an intervention specialist, which meant I would assist students in a classroom taught by another teacher. I thought I might be able to handle this.

I am almost always early, but not this day. I was running late. Maybe it was my subconscious resisting going. To make matters worse, I went to the wrong room and then to another at the opposite end of the building, only to find it was still the wrong room. I was in a frenzy and out of breath by the time I finally got to the right one.

Two young ladies were standing at the teacher's desk. One of them introduced herself as Danielle. I'd seen the name Miss Ackerman on the door but never considered that it would be one of Dustin's friends'. Then I looked over to see Beth, who was the one who carved the pumpkin with his initials and hearts for Halloween to honor his memory.

I exclaimed. "Oh my God. What are you doing here?"

They both replied with a smile, "We are teachers now."

It was such a wonderful and heartwarming encounter. It made my day and as it turned out, I would be in the same class with Danielle for my first and last period.

What are the odds that I would meet up with Dustin's only two classmates and friends that were teachers at Salem High School? They were not only two of his best friends; they were there for me when Dustin passed. They helped me then and are still helping me now.

CHAPTER TWELVE

Image courtesy of Erin Murphy

MISS ME BUT LET ME GO

M Y INTERNAL ALARM USUALLY GOES off around 6:00 AM, but most of the time I stay in bed for a while, using my iPad to get caught up on emails and my Facebook peeps. I am a morning person for the most part, and I was feeling particularly good. At least until I read a post by my friend, Becky. The son of one of her employees was killed in an accident the day before.

Her name was also Michelle, and her son was twenty-three years old. He was the same age as my son would have been then. They could have gone to school together. It was so hard to believe that almost five years had gone by since we lost our Dustin, but it still seemed like yesterday. Now this poor woman had to go through the same thing.

The heartfelt emotion welled up in my chest, and I felt that awful, familiar panic. The memory of the worst day of my life overwhelmed me, and my eyes filled with tears of grief. There was no holding them back. God I missed my Dustin!

Needing a distraction, I put my iPad down and took a few deep breaths. Cleaning, yeah that might take my mind off it. After sweeping the den, I changed the setting on the sweeper to hard surface, and headed into the kitchen. I went around the corner when I noticed the cord was stuck. It had gotten caught under the leg of the refrigerator.

My attempts to get the cord out were unsuccessful, and for the life of me I could not figure out how it got on the other side of the leg. I performed this task routinely, and the cord had never gotten stuck before. "Seriously," I said to my husband, "how can this be?" It just didn't make any sense, and he was as baffled as I was.

We unplugged the sweeper and tried to pull the plug through the space behind the leg, but it was too big. The only thing we could think of was for Dave to pull the fridge out and tip it back while I slipped the cord out from underneath. While working to free it, I noticed piles of hair behind the refrigerator, which was recessed in a maple cabinet. It had been a while since I cleaned behind it, and it needed it badly. Our Ginger was a golden retriever-corgi mix, and she shed a lot. Add another dog and two cats, and well, you get the picture. When we pulled the refrigerator forward, I noticed a piece of paper folded in half. I picked it up and read:

"Miss Me but Let Me Go"
by Edgar A. Guest

When I come to the end of the road
And the sun has set for me,
I want not rites in a gloom-filled room.
Why cry for a soul set free?
Miss me a little - but not too long,
And not with your head bowed low.
Remember the love that we once shared.
Miss me - but let me go.
For this journey we all must take,
And each must go alone.
It's all a part of the Master's Plan,
A step on the road to home.
When you are lonely and sick of heart,
Go to the friends we know,
And bury your sorrow in doing good deeds.
Miss me - but let me go.

His message is clear. Live your life!

EPILOGUE

Losing Dustin dropped me to my knees and broke my will, but I have been so blessed in so many ways. Having my son for seventeen wonderful years was a gift. And I am thankful for the signs that have helped me to get back up and become stronger than ever before. That's what he would have wanted.

Please understand that there will always be some bad times. Anniversaries, birthdays, and holidays can trigger emotions to a heightened state of overwhelming grief. June 30th is and always will be the worst day of my life, and the days immediately following are not much better.

My son passed on the 30th day of June. Calling hours were on July 2nd, which was also my parent's anniversary. The funeral would have been on the third, but that was Dustin's father's birthday, so it was postponed until July 4th. Of course he could not be buried until the following day because of the holiday, so it turned out to be a weeklong nightmare that would be relived again and again. My parent's anniversary, Dave's birthday and the Fourth of July would never be the same.

Panic and anxiety overwhelm me every year from June 30th to July 5th, and this year was no different. My body felt numb and weak.

The uncontrollable sobbing returned again with a vengeance. I spent most of my time in bed.

I awoke from a long nap on the evening of July 5th to find Dave gone, so I called him. He was at the grocery store and had just checked out. Dave asked me if I needed anything and I thought for a moment before I replied, "Chocolate. I need chocolate." (Everybody knows chocolate makes you feel better.)

He decided to stop at the gas station on his way home to pick something up for me. He walked up to the counter and said to the cashier, "My wife needs chocolate."

The cashier smiled at Dave and pointed to the Peanut M&Ms as he replied, "These are buy one, get one free."

"Wow," is all I can say. Thank you, Dustin, for the wonderful tradition with the M&Ms and the ever-lasting memory. My heart was filled with a sense of peace now. It had been a long week, and this was a sign of better times ahead.

I started to write this book to tell everyone how amazing Dustin was and how he continues to reach out. What I ended up doing was writing to connect with others who might be going through the same thing. The unthinkable: the agonizing grief of losing a child.

I think I am ready to finish his story now. It will be titled, "HUFFMAN LEGEND: Run Fast."

After Dustin passed away the utility sink started to get a rust stain for no apparent reason. After several years, it clearly revealed a message. It said, "Hi!"

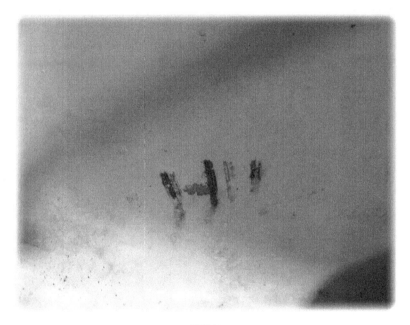

Hi!

Dustin continues to let me know that he will always be with me and that I will see him again.

Peace and Love to you all<3